CONTENTS

New Weapons Technologies and East–West Security in the 1980s

HENRY ROWEN

Many technologies of military relevance are changing; and they interact in complex ways. Undoubtedly some will play a decisive role in future wars, but which? We can make a few predictions with confidence, more which are only inferences, and still more which are mere conjecture.

There are four non-nuclear technologies whose advances are of cardinal importance: (*a*) those for sensing and transmitting signals over a wide range of the electro-magnetic spectrum; (*b*) data processing; (*c*) advances in aerodynamics and propulsion; (*d*) ordnance. The core of technological change lies in the technologies of information, interacting with and amplifying the effectiveness of the other technologies. The first extends our capacity to detect things – targets and non-targets – in an increasingly wide range of environments and to send enormous amounts of data rapidly over long distances. The first and second together make it possible to search for and extract signals from noise, natural and man-made, and to guide vehicles with great precision to targets. The third, together with the others, enables us to build aerodynamic vehicles which can be small and have the ability to fly the 'nap of the earth' for long distances. The fourth makes it possible to tailor more closely the effects of weapons to the characteristics of targets and to the error of delivery; this is especially important for non-nuclear weapons but it is to some extent possible with those which are nuclear.

These changes affect our central concerns: NATO's ability to defend itself at the non-nuclear level and its reliance on nuclear threats; the destructiveness of war and the issue of whether we should be trying to make war more horrible or more humane; our ability to keep open sea lines of communication; the capacity of East and West to project power into third areas; and whether or not we should try to limit the advance of technology.

Ten Propositions

Advances in these technologies support the following propositions:

1. The most elementary proposition is familiar: *if one can see a target* – in the absence of enemy interference – *one will be able to hit it*. And many more targets will be visible from longer distances than in the past: ships, aircraft, air bases, factories, bridges and tanks. This is in marked contrast to the wars of the past, in which hundreds of aircraft might spray thousands of bombs over the landscape in order to get a few on target. Improvements in accuracy now make it possible to reduce the amount of ordnance delivered by a factor of between 100 and 10,000 for a wide range of target types, including soft missile sites, electric power plants, petroleum refineries, steel plants, etc., causing damage that could put such facilities out of action long enough to be significant in important contingencies.

However, if the *attacking* vehicles can be seen, perhaps they too can be hit precisely. This complication suggests a duel which cannot be decided in the abstract. But another proposition applies: defences are almost inevitably imperfect – something can usually penetrate. Now that the chances are good that what gets through will hit, the attacker will find the penetration price worth paying if the target is sufficiently valuable.

1

2. *Forces that operate against a homogeneous background*, especially the sky or the surface of the sea, *will be especially visible and therefore potentially vulnerable.* (This principle of course leaves unsettled the outcome of duels involving aircraft or cruise missiles against ships.) And those that operate against a more heterogeneous background, for example, on land or under the sea, can no longer count on relatively easy concealment. As Andrew Marshall has put it, the sea is no longer black ink.

3. *Less damage to civilians* – especially from the use of high explosives – *will occur as an accidental consequence of war*, because more bombs will hit their targets rather than the neighbourhood, and fewer bombs need to get through to the vicinity of the target. This does not mean, of course, that war will necessarily be more humane, only that a deliberate choice will have to be made if civilians are to be hurt. And again, especially with non-nuclear weapons, such a choice will often be at the expense of directing attack at military targets.

4. *The invaders rather than the invaded will probably be at a disadvantage.* I am not now making the familiar but usually muddled distinction between offensive and defensive weapons. For example, are mobile air defences which are moving forward as part of a combined-arms team offensive or defensive weapons? Clearly both; however, invaders usually have to concentrate their forces and often make themselves visible as they do so; this now makes them more vulnerable. Eric Klippenberg rightly points out that our problem is not offence versus defence – or invading and blocking – in general, but the Warsaw Pact's ability to invade and ours to block. In order to invade they must move; and with improved sensors their movements will be more easily detected. A clear case in point is amphibious landings on unfriendly shores: if the invaded side is equipped with modern surveillance technologies and precision weapons, the invader's prospects are not promising. A less clear but probably valid argument of a similar kind can be applied to blocking ground invasions, especially where the invader's routes of attack are channelled by the terrain. The Pact – if also equipped with weapons of precision – may be able to launch an attack that is both powerful and smaller. Such an attack would generate fewer 'signals' and these signals could be more easily concealed in 'noise' created by exercises, for example, and would be less likely to give NATO a helpful warning time.

5. One reason for uncertainty about the universality of proposition 4 above is that *better information on the location and movement of an opponent's forces, together with more effective means of attack, increases the advantage of moving first.* This creates a danger of pre-emptive strikes. The surprise-attack advantage, which has been evident in the two most recent Arab–Israeli wars, also applies to navies operating in enclosed areas, for example, the Mediterranean. It does not imply an inexorable increase in first-strike instability but, rather, indicates that adaptations are needed to increase warning of and to reduce vulnerability to such pre-emptive strikes.

6. *Advances in technology make some measures to reduce vulnerability easier.* Improved sensors now make it possible to detect small but possibly lethal forces earlier. But heavy dependence on warning and high alertness is risky and costly; it is better to seek a posture that would force a potential first-striker to mount a larger – and noisier – effort. This can be done by using distributed or dispersed systems made up of smaller parts, which are also less likely to be seen, linked by advanced communication technologies. Because increased precision reduces payload needs, and therefore vehicle size in many cases, small vehicles might be substituted for large. This principle applies to aircraft, cruise missiles and remotely piloted vehicles (RPV), and ships.

7. *Distance matters less.* The performance of some high-precision navigation and guidance systems does not vary with distance (the manufacturer of the global positioning system advertises a 30-foot median inaccuracy anywhere). Satellites have eased the problem of gathering information at a distance; the cost of movement by sea has been low for some time, and increased distance adds little to expense; long-haul air transport costs have continued to decline with the advent of jumbo jets. But distance is not irrelevant: the interval between a decision to move forces and their first arrival at the distant terminus and the time it takes to fill a 'pipeline' can be important parameters. The local conditions of the terminus are also very important (for example, whether there are local air defences or a local logistic distribution network), but these factors are more or less independent of distance.

8. *Both the demands on command and control and the potential for extending its scope are increasing greatly.* The necessity of dispersal, concealment and mobility increases the demand for control, while these technologies of information enormously increase the supply possibilities. As Uwe Nerlich and others have pointed out, the main obstacle to realizing these possibilities may be vested organizational interests within services and within separate national governments. There will be a great advantage accruing to those who develop operational procedures for handling large amounts of data and who design procedures for information handling and decision-making which match well to technological and human capacities.

9. *Advanced technology is necessary but not sufficient.*[1] Technology is most powerful in the hands of those who develop and adopt an effective doctrine for its use. The tank had been around for twenty-five years before it was first used with decisive effect. It required years of doctrinal development by Fuller, Liddell-Hart, De Gaulle and others before its full potential was realized by Guderian. The German success with tanks was not based on superior technology but on a superior concept of how to use a not-very-advanced technology. We should expect to see this lesson repeated.

10. A technological lead is extremely useful, but *size of forces still matters a great deal.* Some of the technological developments are partially offset by each other, and this gives an advantage to the side with the most weapons. Although the Soviet Union lags in some of these developments she is ahead in others (for example, mobile SAM and deployed cruise missiles). The winner of the future – as in the past – will often be the side that runs out of weapons and troops second. Despite superior NATO information technologies, the Soviet Union might manage simply to blast through with enough tanks, artillery and people.

---

[1] Does the Vietnam War demonstrate that it is not even necessary? Perhaps, but the fairly modern Soviet SAM defences were undoubtedly useful in the North, and Soviet-made artillery and, in the end, tanks made a great difference in the South.

Some Inferences

If these changes, vigorously pursued, promise a relative improvement in NATO's ability to block an invasion and to do so while reducing collateral damage, it would seem that they would be unambiguously a good thing. Consider, however, the furore in the United States and Germany over the neutron bomb. The neutron bomb has been attacked on the grounds that it is (*a*) too destructive and (*b*) not destructive enough. Those of the first view claim that such weapons are too destructive because the effect of neutrons is not well enough known, or declare that radioactive fallout may be increased. Those of the second view declare that the gap between nuclear and non-nuclear arms has been narrowed and that the reduction in civilian damage makes the use of these weapons tempting, more likely and therefore dangerous because, once nuclear weapons are used, escalation follows.

This dispute bears on the potential role of improved non-nuclear technologies. Advanced non-nuclear technologies will cause less indiscriminate destruction. Should we reject them on the grounds that to use them will be too tempting? Not if we believe that we face a formidable adversary against whom we need a capacity to act which is militarily effective without being suicidal. The second part of this requirement, a capacity to take non-suicidal action, is even more important in an alliance than in a single state. Political decisions are more likely to be taken if the criterion of achieving a desired military effect within the constraint of limited civilian damage can be met.

Modern non-nuclear technologies can do more: for some missions they can substitute for nuclear weapons. Where this is the case, there is no blurring of the distinction between nuclear and non-nuclear – the firebreak between non-nuclear and nuclear choices is widened. This can hardly be in dispute. But it does not follow that a large-scale substitution of non-nuclear for nuclear weapons must come next. Firstly, although the Soviet Union lags in the development of technologies of information, she does not seem to lag in fielding useful equipment and in making needed adaptations, and NATO's ability to maintain an effective lead is uncertain. Secondly, whatever the potential for improving the non-nuclear blocking capacity, the need to discourage a nuclear attack on Europe remains urgent. Thirdly, more vehicles will be genuinely dual-capable – i.e. nuclear and non-nuclear – because the effectiveness of small non-nuclear packages is higher. Cruise missiles and RPV provide perhaps the best examples.

Defending Europe

Unless NATO continues to make changes to reduce its vulnerability, the Pact's surprise-attack capacity will grow; it may already be able to mount a powerful attack without extensive reinforcement, and such an attack could give NATO little usable warning. In contrast, if NATO's posture is resilient to sudden attack, the Pact will have to build up and concentrate, and it could be vulnerable during this process if NATO has invested in improved battlefield surveillance, mobile artillery, air-delivered area munitions, improved anti-tank weapons, etc. Despite the growing difficulty of penetrating modern air defences, much more effective attack against fixed targets (for example, bridges and command centres) might be managed in order to disrupt the forward movement and supply of Pact forces. On the battlefield, improved target-acquisition technology and the use of RPV, drones and precision weapons (including advanced area munitions) could serve to blunt a Soviet combined-arms attack, at least to the extent of disrupting it, perhaps with substantial direct destruction. (There is a good deal of disagreement about the best way to achieve these ends.)[2]

The Soviet Union, of course, is adopting these technologies, and (given her higher material production rates) her inventories of advanced weapons may grow rapidly. She is investing heavily not only in the ground-force equipment about which we hear so much – tanks, self-propelled artillery, anti-tank weapons and armoured personnel carriers – but also in surveillance, electronic countermeasures and command-and-control capacities. She is also investing much more than before in tactical aircraft with offensive capacities. These are equipped with modern precision munitions,

including those with area coverage, and they will present a much greater threat of disruption and damage to NATO forces than in the past. Mobile air defences and improved low-altitude radar coverage have become urgent for NATO force improvement.

Defence of the flanks may be especially affected by the increased vulnerability of sea and air forces noted in Proposition 2 above. In a Soviet attacking force these components could be subject to high attrition. So also might some of the Western forces moving in reinforcement of the flanks. The lesson, yet again, is to avoid 'giantism'. A multiplicity of smaller units will permit earlier arrival of some reinforcements on the flank – an important political desideratum – as well as providing more difficult targets for Soviet attack.

It is natural to speculate not only about the implications of these developments for the Alliance *vis-à-vis* the Warsaw Pact but also about the implications for intra-Alliance relations of changes in information technology. One should not, however, conclude that increased US technical dominance in the Alliance will be a consequence. These technologies are dynamic; the United States has a lead in some, but others in the West are not far behind. They are ubiquitous – they will pervade both civil and military sectors. It is important for the West to stay ahead, and fortunately it seems to have an advantage in economic organization, and even in culture, in these technologies.

It is difficult to see major implications for large states relative to small states in these developments, but other distinctions may emerge clearly. For instance, people who live on islands will find it easier to protect themselves against invasion, whereas those who depend on unimpeded movement of shipping may find themselves at a disadvantage. (There are lessons for Japan and for the NATO countries here.)

Because the prospects for action at a distance are improved, the possibility of an effective non-nuclear attack across political boundaries is more likely, at least against peripheral bases and war-supporting industry in an attacker's homeland. Such a possibility raises the familiar problem of escalation or, more precisely, widening of the war. Those who hold that no serious use of nuclear weapons should be contemplated because of the risk of a nuclear

[2] For a discussion of differing European and American views on how to conduct tactical air operations under modern conditions, see Stephen Canby *The Contribution of Tactical Air-power in Countering a Blitz: European Perceptions* (Washington DC: Technology Service Corporation, May 1977).

holocaust and that non-nuclear cross-border attacks on military forces or war-production facilities of an attacker are too dangerous are, in effect, in favour of giving an attacker an unconditional promise that his homeland will be safe. Such a stance is not promising for stability in Europe. It does at least appear that there can be a *choice* between the use of nuclear weapons – on the battlefield only, say, or even on NATO territory only – and non-nuclear use on Warsaw Pact territory.

NATO has a critical dependence on sea lines of communication. Alliance shipping must continue to operate; oil must be transported and rein-forcements sent to Europe. Soviet ocean sur-veillance is improving rapidly through the use of satellites with data links, increased access to overseas bases for reconnaissance aircraft and information-gathering ships. These, together with cruise missiles and long-range supersonic *Backfire* bombers, make the Soviet Union much more effective in sea attack. In a surprise attack, particularly, she might score important successes.

There are good reasons, however, why NATO should not be too gloomy about the prospect of keeping these lines of communication open. In the absence of a large accretion of territory, or bases in better positions, the Soviet Union will continue to have only restricted access to the open oceans, and barriers with sensors, sub-marines and 'smart' mines can make her transits costly. Air-defence barriers can also deter her aircraft. Much of her information-gathering and peripheral attack abilities might not survive long in a serious conflict. (Nor, incidentally, should the West count on its own surviving any longer.) The Soviet surface fleet is likely to be very vulnerable beyond the umbrella of Soviet land-based air defences. In short, a prolonged struggle to keep sea lines open seems likely to be successful for NATO. What is more worrying is the disruption which the Soviet Union could cause to these lines during the critical opening period of a European conflict – which might also be the closing period if she managed a rapid advance.

Competition and Conflict in Third Areas
Skill in deploying small forces rapidly and striking with high accuracy over very long ranges is clearly increasing. Commando raids of the kind carried out at Entebbe and Mogadishu are examples of one type; others are the rapid movement of Cubans to Angola and the air and sea supply by both sides to the Middle East in the 1973 war.

The Soviet Union is achieving sustained growth in her ability to project power into areas remote from her borders, and particular progress has been made in her long-range airlift. Some years ago she was unable to sustain a small airlift to Peru; now she conducts long-range operations to distant places as a matter of routine. This development is not so much the product of a major technological advance (although cumulative improvements in aircraft design, engines and command and control are important) as of investment and learning in a new line of work. This is another illustration of the point already made that it is often not a technological breakthrough that is of decisive importance but learning how to use technologies that are evolving incrementally.

The growing capacity of the Soviet Union to operate in third areas raises many issues which go beyond the scope of a discussion centred on new technologies. But in one region at least, the Middle East, the transfer of modern arms is occurring on a scale large enough to warrant comment. Some of these weapons are simple to use; others, such as the F-15, are extraordinarily complex and will require a large support system and foreign help for many years to come. The 1973 war showed how effective many of these weapons can be, how rapidly regional balances can be altered by the transfer of advanced weapons, and the high intensity of conflict and rate of material usage that can result.

Possession of advanced weapons by regional powers increases the potential cost to outsiders of intervention as, for instance, the Soviet Union threatened in the Middle East in 1973. Still more costly would be intervention against the future regional possessors of nuclear weapons.

How Constraining is Cost?
It is often remarked that some of the new weapons are impressively effective but priced out of reach. The unit cost of some modern weapons is indeed very high, but some of the most costly weapons may not be the most useful ones in the years ahead. For example, it has been decided not to go ahead with the $100-million-per-item B-1 bomber; the US Administration

is trying to keep Congress from going ahead with a $2-billion nuclear-powered aircraft carrier; tanks costing $1 million or more apiece are not likely to be produced in large numbers. In short, the changes that are taking place affecting weapon costs are more complex than is implied by the observation that everything is getting much more costly; a shift towards less costly alternatives is also evident. In contrast, the costs of a given capability in information technologies continue to decline rapidly, especially with data processing.

New technology merely offers a wider range of choice; the old alternatives do not disappear, and, if old is better than new within a given budget, it can still be chosen. Complaints about the high cost of some of the new weapons largely come down to complaints and worries about the size of defence budgets. Given the impressive build-up in the East, these worries seem justified and need to be faced.

To those who see advances in technical knowledge as increasing the potential for destruction, and therefore its reality, technology is bad and should be stopped. If not stopped by agreement with adversaries, perhaps it should be stopped by unilateral action. The alternative, and on the whole dominant, view is not that technology is good *per se* or that if something can be made it should be, but rather that advances in technology give us a wider range of choices. And more choices, by and large, are better than fewer.[3]

Should we try to stop some of these non-nuclear technologies? Some proposals have been made to this effect – for example, the barring of

---

[3] This does not necessarily mean that we should go all the way to develop a technology before thinking about whether we really need it. For example, it makes sense to stop and think hard about some types of recombinant DNA research, or nuclear reactor technologies that necessarily require the wide circulation of nuclear explosive materials. After thinking about it, we might sensibly decide to impose some restrictions on what is developed.

napalm and area-distributed sub-munitions. Many current versions of these weapons lack delivery accuracy, which reduces their military effectiveness and increases the likelihood of collateral damage. (Even so, it is doubtful whether they are as indiscriminately damaging as the iron bombs that used to be so widely scattered.) But area weapons being developed will be more precise in delivery, and therefore not as subject to the legitimate charge of causing inadvertent damage.

The principal legitimate reason for prohibiting a military technology, in my view, is that it might cause indiscriminate damage. Because these technologies offer increases in precision and control they should be encouraged. In addition, most emerge from advances so integral to the fabric of modern industrial development that it would be virtually impossible to put workable agreed contraints on them – although we might manage to slow ourselves down.

To the extent that technological changes and changes in force disposition (especially in the East) are increasing the advantage of pre-emption, the Mutual and Balanced Force Reductions (MBFR) negotiations might usefully concentrate on measures to increase warning of attack preparations, reducing 'noise' through restrictions on manoeuvres, and notification of movements in the region and deployments into it.

It should be evident that the Alliance depends crucially on the new technologies. Certainly a failure to press ahead vigorously will leave us at a growing disadvantage. In some of them – microelectronics and computers for instance – the West has an advantage that it is not likely to be transient. We can identify the technologies that are of cardinal importance and in which we have – or can acquire – a comparative advantage, and drive this advantage as far as possible. We do not have many areas left in which we have an edge over the East, and we need to make the most of what we have.

The Political Choices

UWE NERLICH

Over the last five years unprecedented efforts have been underway to improve Western theatre capabilities. Postural changes may eventually turn out to be significant, though the current policy-formation process bears little similarity to earlier major efforts to change NATO's military posture. The 'new look' in the mid-1950s was an extension of strategic force improvements; the policy of 'conventional options' in the early 1960s was based on new manpower requirements rather than new technologies. Recent advances, on the other hand, were stimulated above all by maturing technologies in a wide range of theatre applications. No new basic defence concept has yet emerged, but some rather comprehensive approaches have developed. Their increasing acceptance within the Alliance may eventually allow political choices to be taken into consideration where incrementalism would otherwise have had its way yet again.

There are three types of new comprehensive approaches. In terms of functions a methodology of target-engagement processes began to develop in order to relate different defence functions and corresponding technologies on various theatre levels. One standard format of this employment cycle is (a) target acquisition, (b) information processing, (c) delivery, and (d) munition. Special efforts went into covering the various classes of target systems as well as the requirements for combined-arms combat.

In terms of implications there is now recognition of the fact that full exploitation of new technologies will be possible only along with changes in tactics, force structure, strategy (nuclear/non-nuclear nexus) and on the basis of the requirements for a plausible range of contingencies, some of which were not considered NATO contingencies in the past.

In terms of long-term requirements new mechanisms for early assessment of common needs as well as available technological options have developed across the Atlantic, and promise to avoid the immobilism as well as the compartmentalization which usually results from established procedures. In fact they have already begun to feed back into national defence bureaucracies so as to stimulate more internal co-ordination.

In all three approaches these changes are only beginning, but they are encouraging. While results are but modest, they combine with a growing awareness of NATO's postural deficiencies, as well as with perception of a maturing Soviet threat against Western Europe, to induce the new Administration in Washington to continue previous efforts and, furthermore, to launch vigorous defence improvement programmes in NATO.

If sustained efforts are made, there is a chance of improving NATO's theatre capabilities in ways which might deny the more plausible Soviet offensive options. Military stability could be achieved even in Central Europe as a result of appropriately reorientated defence policies. While military stability would affect political expectations in Western Europe significantly, there is of course no way of escape from the Alliance's inherent nuclear dilemmas. Yet – in the context of a policy of nuclear de-emphasis – they may to some extent cease to be a constant source of tension inside the Alliance.

While new technologies were an important catalyst during the process which led to NATO's current initiatives, there is no singularly dominant technology, nor will any of the new technologies drive organizational and doctrinal developments. In fact technological change will be but incremental unless it combines with changes in force structure, tactics and strategy, i.e., with changes which require painful decisions within a number of independent defence establishments. There is little accepted wisdom in Western governments about which combined changes of equipment, force structure, tactics and strategy are most promising. In fact there is still an enormous lack of analysis and dissemination. Moreover, even if appropriate concepts and policies emerge, there is no machinery yet to implement them in any coherent fashion.

Controversies are no longer over basic objectives but over improvement programmes. Complete reliance on improved theatre nuclear forces (TNF) is no longer regarded as an answer, although TNF improvements are part of the more general improvement effort. Nor is there political support for what Bernard Brodie has labelled the 'CWE philosophy' (i.e., the preference for conventional options only), although reduced dependence on nuclear capabilities is regarded as an important goal of Western defence improvements. Simplistic concepts of sweeping change have been replaced by an evolutionary notion of improvement which is intended to strike a balance between the kind of radicalism which is favoured by some politicians and the incrementalism which tends to be the preference of military bureaucracies.

In the past, major changes in NATO's military posture were primarily understood in terms of how they affected the distribution of control, risk or burden inside the Alliance. Concepts of change were above all vehicles of political interest. What was seen to be at stake was the way a nation defined its principal relations inside the Alliance. Defence was thus a key element of high politics – a practice which often prevented major issues of defence improvement from being decided on purely military grounds.[1] Issues of force improvement in NATO will not develop primarily in terms of conflicting national interests, but rather in terms of intra-govern-

mental conflicts with all sorts of transnational coalitions, especially on service levels (where traditional devices such as restricted data-exchange agreements will help to protect parochial interests). It will be very hard, therefore, to implement policies of force improvement in terms of intra-governmental co-ordination without high-level backing. It will be hard also to do so without again lifting these issues to levels where they become nothing but vehicles of political interest. Thus it will be important to fashion political choices in terms of comprehensive intermediate objectives which allow coalitions of support to be generated. Major force-posture changes are no longer identified with favoured or abhorred notions of regional order. The biggest obstacles are likely to be organizational interests in a national context, faced with the conflicting objectives of drawing the Soviet Union into a more co-operative system and of matching growing Soviet military capabilities.[2] Governments will have to choose between major procurement programmes which help to reduce unemployment and possibilities of improving military effectiveness.[3] In addition some will want to protect markets or high-technology organizations, or may give higher priority to balanced budgets.

Technology as a Policy Tool
There is recent evidence that new technologies can stimulate efforts to change theatre capabilities. But while new strategic force options derive largely from new technology, major theatre force improvements require complex decisions combining changes of force structure, strategy, tactics and equipment. As a rule new tech-

---

[1] It took six years (and the withdrawal of France from NATO) to get NATO to adopt MC 14/3, and at least as many years again before the new doctrine began to have a significant effect on NATO's deployment plans. Yet the chances of implementing a policy of flexible response in terms of what was acheivable in the 1960s had already faded away in the early 1960s – years before NATO came round to adopting MC 14/3.

[2] While NATO's defence improvement programmes were vigorous American initiatives, one of the key issues around which internal controversies over the new American basic security document, the so-called PRM-10, are said to have evolved was whether or not the Soviet Union had achieved conventional superiority in Central Europe. This would seem to suggest that important segments of the new Administration consider a major policy statement to this effect as politically undesirable in view of the fragile nature of continuing detente efforts.
[3] For example, some of the more recent West German procurement decisions (*Tornado* or Type 122 frigates) have been taken primarily for economic reasons (e.g. job-creating programmes) and to the detriment of improved theatre defence capabilities. Low procurement of ammunition has similar reasons: ammunition production is not labour-intensive.

nologies will be adopted on the basis of what appears compatible with existing force structures, strategy and tactics. General beliefs about technological dynamics influence Western policy-making on defence issues mainly in two ways: in terms of effect on stability, and in terms of possible compensatory utilities. Both beliefs are deep-rooted, and both date back to the 1950s.

The doctrine of stability first emerged on the strategic level in relation to potential first-strike instabilities, then, in the European context, in relation to escalatory risks. Until a few years ago the latter was essentially an American pre-occupation which constantly irritated West Europeans, concerned about what might become of the American commitment. However, West European views have developed lately to adopt the doctrine of stability in rather bizarre ways: in spite of the constant increase of Soviet offensive options, the West Europeans want European force relationships to be codified in terms of allegedly existing stability. The talks on Mutual and Balanced Force Reductions (MBFR) helped to shape these outlooks more than anything else. Major Western efforts to offset Soviet offensive capabilities by major force improvements are widely considered a threat to stability – seldom expressed explicitly for fear of jeopardizing the Vienna negotiations. Strangely, this applies primarily to new technologies and their possible exploitation.

The current debate in Western Europe (notably in West Germany) on enhanced-radiation (ER) weapons (the so-called 'neutron bombs') has all the ingredients of this new West European approach to 'stability'. For many years West Europeans – West Germans above all – have stressed both the indispensability of nuclear weapons for use against massive tank offensives and the vital importance of avoiding collateral damage. In recent years the gap between Soviet offensive capabilities and Western anti-tank capabilities has widened. Various options for improved theatre nuclear weapons have been studied in NATO for several years in order to meet West European interests. In terms of intended effectiveness, as well as collateral damage, ER weapons are a major improvement over existing weapons. But once the US government moved towards procurement, West Europeans were outraged. Some even argued that stability should be achieved through current

MBFR negotiations and, since introducing ER weapons would jeopardize MBFR, they are a threat to stability.

This is not a singular event; nor is it confined to fringe positions. A European doctrine on the destabilizing effects of force improvement will be a major factor in years to come. While the 'Neo-Luddites' – as Albert Wohlstetter has called these protagonists of 'stability' – may eventually do little harm in American strategic policy, they appear strangely self-defeating in a West European context, where the compensatory utilities of new technologies are much greater. For many years American notions of stability, which had originated in a central balance context, had never been applicable to the European theatre. Now for the first time the Soviet threat against Western Europe is maturing and makes non-reinforced massive campaigns conceptually comparable to first-strike instabilities on the strategic plane; yet a disposition has emerged in Western Europe to consider the present balance as stable, and possible remedies as destabilizing.

Along with this doctrine of stability, which claims that technology is driving arms races, there is a doctrine of compensation, which claims that technology can be a substitute in a wide variety of trade-offs. This doctrine also originated in the United States but, unlike the other, it is characterized by technological optimism. In general terms it scarcely boosts defence policies in Western Europe to the extent that it does in the United States at times, and in fact most versions of technological optimism prove rather to militate against prudent modernization in Western Europe. One can distinguish two kinds of compensatory approach. Reductionist approaches trade new technology for elements of the existing posture – usually American elements. Balancing approaches are meant to offset existing imbalances – usually Soviet advantages.

Reductionist approaches have been manifold – some genuine, some caused by West European suspicions, some both. One type of reductionist trade-off would be technology for manpower. While this may not be confined to US forces, it is widely understood to mean mainly that.[4]

---

[4] As early as 1967 the Subcommittee on National Security and International Operations to the Committee on Government Operations (chaired by Senator Jackson)

Other intended or alleged trade-offs would concern the deterrence link of American strategic forces to Western Europe, the participation of West Europeans in nuclear control or in the military market or, more generally, the American commitment to Western Europe's defence. While it is probably true that 'the United States stands to gain most from procurement of the new weapons',[5] West European propensities for suspecting that some applications of technology are extreme or trivial tend at times to stand in the way of serious progress.[6]

Offsetting Soviet imbalances is seen in terms of overall force relationships (quantity v. quality or offensive v. defensive) or of specific Soviet advantages or of unbalanced results of negotiations (which are justified by technological superiority). However, in the matter of overall force relationships it is often ignored 'that the balance already assumes a degree of Western technological superiority'[7] and that 'Soviet forces have achieved approximate qualitative parity in conventional technology'.[8] While more extreme views regard new technologies as equalizers, the important consideration is which specific offensive options one could deny by what new means. This is a matter not of beliefs, but of analysis.

Along with these two compensatory approaches one might mention what could be labelled the mobilizing approach which claims new challenges[9] or new opportunities. The more simplistic view is that new technology is a panacea in the sense that one can do things now which were not feasible in the past; most of the earlier PGM literature was of this kind. A more sophisticated view holds that 'new technology should be viewed as releasing the constraints upon present operating practices, rather than, as now, being constrained by them'.[10] While the first view tends to ignore constraints (i.e., doctrine and organization) and the second hopes to change them, there is a third position which states that 'technology is now catching up with doctrine and making it easier to implement. What is needed is the gradual introduction of weapons and plans for their use that are better adapted politically to the purposes that have been recognized in NATO doctrine'.[11] While complex changes involving doctrine and organization will be necessary in the longer run, the latter position seems to fit West European views on force modernization most easily.

As with strategic issues in the past, beliefs about technology (in terms of both stability and compensation) play an important role in force modernization. At times they cause markedly divergent perspectives. Beliefs about stability tend to retard modernization on both sides of the Atlantic, but beliefs about trade-offs often stimulate American efforts, whereas – for precisely the same reasons – they tend to make West Europeans cautious. This disparity is strongly reinforced by two things: institutional response and the dominance of the nuclear system in NATO.

The Neo-Luddite contentions about technological dynamism contrast oddly with the frustrations of non-conservative force planners. If anything, both are falsified by institutional

---

stated that 'with the advance of technology it may be possible to make some redeployment of combat garrisons and their logistic and support elements on the Continent without reducing the capability needed'. (*The Atlantic Alliance: Unfinished Business*, Washington DC: USGPO, 1967, p. 7). A rather extreme example would be how the Los Alamos concept for a radical TNF modernization was sold in the press some years ago: 'American bomblets and German bodies'.

[5] Richard Burt, *New Weapons Technologies: Debate and Directions*, Adelphi Paper No. 126 (London: IISS, 1976) p. 21.

[6] E.g. the scope of the NPG study on new technologies (the MIT study) was severely narrowed by some West European views of this kind.

[7] Kenneth Hunt, 'New Technology and the European Theatre' in Geoffrey Kemp, Robert L. Pfaltzgraff, Jr and Uri Ra'anan, *The Other Arms Race* (Lexington, Mass.: Lexington Books, D.C. Heath, 1975), p. 109.

[8] Phillip A. Karber, *Evolution of the Central European Balance* (McLean, Va.: BDM Corp., 14 June 1977), p. 3.

[9] See, for example, the Rumsfeld Statement: 'The technological revolution has caused the paradoxical effect of reviving, albeit in a modified form, the geopolitical character of the world of pre-nuclear years'. (*Annual Defence Department Report FY* 1978, Washington DC: USGPO, 17 January 1977), p. 13.

[10] Steven Canby, *The Alliance and Europe: Part IV. Military Doctrine and Technology*, Adelphi Paper No. 109 (London: IISS, 1975), p. 13. See also Barry M. Blechman *et al.*, 'Toward a New Consensus in Defence Policy' in Henry Owen and Charles L. Schultze (eds), *Setting National Priorities: The Next Ten Years* (Washington DC: The Brookings Institution, 1976), p. 127.

[11] Henry S. Rowen and Albert Wohlstetter, 'Varying Response with Circumstance' in Johan J. Holst and Uwe Nerlich (eds), *Beyond Nuclear Deterrence: New Aims, New Arms* (New York: Crane Russak, 1977), pp. 228f. See also Laurence Martin, 'Flexibility in Tactical Nuclear Response', *ibid.*

realities: 'Military history of the past half century is studded with institutions which have managed to dodge the challenge of the obvious'.[12] While it may be true that technological advance is 'the most rapidly changing influence on defence decisions',[13] it tends rather to strengthen conservative institutional behaviour. As Edward Katzenbach has observed, there is an inherent dilemma: while lead-times are increasing so as to allow for timely institutional adaptations, lag-times (i.e., the period between innovation and a successful institutional response) are increasing as well.[14] Thus the distressed conclusion of a commission charged with recommending a more national organization of government (the Murphy Commission) that the 'same organizational factors that produce adverse outcomes within the present system stand in the way of attempts to restructure the system'.[15]

The institutional behaviour of defence establishments in the United States and in West European countries differs significantly.[16] While the American armed forces were extremely isolated until World War II, they have since had increasing exposure; on the other hand, armed forces in Western Europe not only became increasingly confined to the European theatre but have been in constant trouble escaping from their various crises of identity. Throughout the 1950s and beyond the United States became the only agent of major change, and there was no rationale in Western Europe for shaping national forces outside the Alliance structure. Moreover, while on the one hand the American

R&D base was overwhelming, massive American military aid to Western Europe also provided disincentives for autonomous innovation on a large scale. West European defence policy thus displays essentially the same inertia which operated in the American system. But at the same time there are much fewer internal innovative impulses in a considerably more constrained institutional setting, and the innovative inputs that do occur are mainly mediated through NATO, towards which most West European defence establishments have developed a reflex of caution and reserve.

The Prohibitive Nature of the Nuclear System

Institutional maladjustment to technical change is thus the rule rather than the exception. Yet since the early 1950s this problem has acquired new dimensions: incongruence of means, doctrine and organization are more and more often carried forward to future weapons generations. The single most important change was the simultaneous introduction of H-bombs into the strategic arsenal and atomic weapons into theatre forces. As Bernard Brodie observed at this juncture: 'We are thus faced with the necessity of exploring the implications of the new type when we have not yet succeeded in comprehending the implications of the old'.[17]

This is not a matter of poor intentions, but rather of organizational behaviour. To quote Bernard Brodie again: 'When we recall that both sides prior to World War I failed utterly, with incalculable resulting costs, to adjust adequately in their thinking to something as evolutionary as the machine gun ... we can hardly be sanguine about the adjustments likely to be made to such quantum change as that represented by developments in nuclear weapons. This is ... simply to question where the motivation and pressure is to come from that will cause incredibly busy men, advanced in rank and experience, to preoccupy themselves with basic issues which are confounding in the extreme and which must play havoc with special service interests and previous indoctrination'.[18]

While the introduction of nuclear weapons into theatre forces was one of the major boosts

---

[12] Edward L. Katzenbach, 'The Horse Cavalry in the Twentieth Century' in *Public Policy* (1958), pp. 120–49, reprinted in Robert J. Art and Kenneth N. Waltz (eds), *The Use of Force* (Boston: Little Brown, 1971), pp. 277–97.
[13] Barry Blechman, *op. cit.* in note 10.
[14] Katzenbach, *op. cit.* in note 12, p. 277.
[15] *Commission on the Organization of the Government for the Conduct of Foreign Policy* (Murphy Commission), Vol. 4, Appendix K: 'Adequacy of Current Organization: Defence and Arms Control', (Washington DC: USGPO, 1975), p. 214.
[16] While there is a lack of comparative studies, some more specialized studies provide considerable insight. See, for example, Bernard Udis, *Adjustment of High Technology Organizations to Reduced Military Spending: The Western European Experience* (prepared for the National Science Foundation. Main Report, October 1974). See also Graham T. Allison and Frederic A. Morris, 'Precision Guidance for NATO: Justification and Constraints' in Holst/Nerlich, *op. cit.* in note 11, pp. 215–20.

[17] Bernard Brodie, *Military Implications of Nuclear Weapons Developments* (Santa Monica, Calif.: Rand Corporation, P-444, 30 October 1953), p. 2.
[18] *Ibid.*, pp. 4f.

11

for the structural development of NATO in the 1950s, it was also the single most important failure in Allied force planning since NATO had been formed, and we still suffer from the lack of comprehension almost a quarter of a century later. The American military leadership then was still preoccupied with studying the implications of the conventional war in Korea,[19] and the introduction of nuclear weapons into theatre forces occurred under conditions of nuclear scarcity as well as absolute priority for strategic forces. These factors were conducive to regarding nuclear weapons as 'just another limited addition to an already large arsenal at their disposal – and not as a weapon which might itself revolutionize ground warfare. It may account for what on the surface appears to be an effort to fit atomic weapons into existing ground force organization and doctrine with a minimum dislocation'.[20] Thus the World War II type of organization remained essentially unchanged, while theatre nuclear weapons became that 'strange hermaphrodite creature, half HE and half atomic . . . having all the limitation of the former with only half the potentiality of the latter'.[21]

Suggestions that the employment of nuclear weapons in land warfare should be considered 'not as weapons of opportunity, but as the main source of shock power, . . . as something whose power the infantry might exploit'[22] were of but marginal importance.[23] Yet while American doctrine and organization for theatre warfare remained largely unchanged, theatre nuclear weapons were introduced at an increasing pace – reflecting the change from nuclear scarcity to nuclear plenty during the 1950s. Again, while US military organization was only marginally affected, the introduction of theatre nuclear

weapons profoundly shaped the Allied command structure.[24]

By the time NATO had acquired theatre nuclear weapons roughly at present levels (implying profound changes in doctrine and organization, inevitable for American as well as West European forces), the United States tried to turn the clock back towards conventional defence – without a change of implementation and without changing the nuclear posture either. NATO force planning has suffered from these developments ever since. Conventional defence continues to be seen in the shadow of nuclear weapons, without any effort made to marry conventional and nuclear options, and nuclear warfare continues to offer hardly any military options because, until quite recently, the United States preferred not to exploit new nuclear technologies which would have allowed major tactical nuclear weapon (TNW) modernization. The doctrine of stability had caught the Alliance half-way, leaving NATO with the worst of both worlds.

While NATO is now trying to assess the implications of new technologies for the 1980s and 1990s it still fails to comprehend the implications of that major change in the early 1950s and everything that has stemmed from it.[25] In fact NATO continues to avoid the issue. While both nuclear and non-nuclear technologies are being studied in the Nuclear Planning Group (NPG), they are discussed essentially in separation. It is the combined effect of improved nuclear and non-nuclear theatre capabilities which could neutralize the matured Soviet threat against Central Europe. Yet the only comprehensive approach in NATO is geared towards possible

---

[19] H. A. DeWeerd, *Atomic Weapons and Ground Combat: The Search for Organization and Doctrine* (Santa Monica, Calif.: The Rand Corporation, P-497, 12 March 1954), pp. 4f.
[20] *Ibid.*, p. 6.
[21] *Ibid.*
[22] *Ibid.*, p. 9.
[23] It may be significant that the British Defence Ministry's White Paper of 1954 speaks of employing conventional forces to exploit atomic and advanced weapons rather than the other way around – a doctrine which the Soviet Union eventually adopted some ten years later. (cf. A. A. Sidorenko, *The Offensive* (Moscow: Military Publishing House, 1970), translated and published under the auspices of the US Air Force. Washington DC, 1973), pp. 41–5.

[24] As Alastair Buchan has observed: 'the fact that the command structure must be American controlled is partly a consequence of the failure of the European allies nearly twenty years ago to think through the consequences of permitting the introduction of American tactical nuclear weapons into Europe'. *The End of the Postwar Era: A New Balance of World Power* (London: Weidenfeld & Nicolson, 1974), p. 235.
[25] To quote a former senior NATO commander: 'The commander today possesses little more than military judgement to apply to the tasks of determining how theater nuclear weapons can help him achieve his objective. He lacks analytical tools.' (George J. Eade, 'An Examination of NATO's Theater Nuclear Element: Strategy and Capabilities' unpublished manuscript, February 1977, p. 3.5). Oddly enough, he also lacks improvements in non-nuclear technology – for information processing for nuclear employments, for example.

substitutions of new conventional means for existing nuclear weapons – an important though narrowly confined subject.

There has been some doctrinal progress recently: in the past West Europeans tended to regard major conventional improvement efforts as undermining the nuclear posture. Now it is widely recognized that it is only through improved conventional defence that viable theatre nuclear options can be generated and maintained. And it is only in combination with nuclear options that major conventional improvement efforts can provide a defence posture which can be expected to deny Soviet offensive options. Thus the crucial thing is to 'combine nuclear and conventional weapons in ways more subtly graduated than the mere sequence of conventional first and nuclear afterward'.[26] But while this basic requirement for conventional force improvements is increasingly recognized in prudent advice,[27] official thinking is still dominated by the notion of 'thresholds', which is unspecifiable operationally yet serves to freeze the kind of comprehensive approach which has been normal in Soviet strategic policy ever since the 1960s.

The Need for a New Posture

For many years the Alliance has been widely perceived as a kind of unitary system – to such an extent that the alienation of some member states as a result of the selective co-operation of others was regarded as a more serious penalty than lack of efficiency, that major countries like West Germany defined their military identity in terms of NATO contributions, and that the withdrawal of France from NATO was considered an earth-shaking event. Yet today it is obvious that 'there is really no such thing as a NATO defence posture, only a collection of heterogeneous national postures'.[28] In fact it may seem odd that at the very moment NATO seems to be increasingly deprived of what was believed to be coherence, one of the chief architects of the current improvement effort, Robert Komer, claims that 'all Allies, including the United States, need to start "thinking NATO", rather than thinking primarily in terms of national programmes, while paying mostly lip service to common goals'.[29]

While Allied governments now face the task of undoing twenty-odd years of seemingly inappropriate force planning, it should be taken into account that the shortcomings were to some extent the by-product of a system which allowed common institutions, and thus political stability, to flourish more easily than they would have done had military requirements been the dominant priority. Military technology plays an important part in this, not as an engine of transformation but rather because it preserves conditions. As Katzenbach has observed, 'weapons are adopted – apparently in great part because of the appeal they make to a set of social values'.[30]

In force-planning terms the failure to comprehend the implications of introducing nuclear weapons into NATO may indeed have been disastrous. Yet – up to a point – nuclear technology allowed military security to be of prime importance in the West without the full price being paid. It thus provided the Alliance with the best of both worlds – highly developed common institutions without seriously conflicting social goals.[31] The main characteristics of the system were as follows. It was based on a dominant threat perception, but the Soviet threat was seen in a kind of generalized and depoliticized manner, and limited to potential overt aggression against NATO territory.[32] It displayed a degree

[26] Laurence Martin, *op. cit.* in note 11, p. 262.
[27] See, for example, *ibid.*; Kenneth Hunt, *op. cit.* in note 7, p. 122; Canby, *op. cit.* in note 10, p. 5; Holst, 'Flexible Options in Alliance Strategy', and Peter Stratmann, 'Limited Options, Escalation, and the Central Region', in Holst/Nerlich, pp. 271, 239–54.
[28] Robert W. Komer, 'Ten Suggestions for Rationalizing NATO', *Survival*, March/April 1977, p. 68.
[29] *Ibid.*, pp. 68f.
[30] *Op. cit.* in note 12, p. 297. Incidentally the same observation is made from the Soviet camp – only a little more clumsily: 'This interaction is socially caused . . . No matter how developed science and technology may be, their use is determined by social and class interests'. (N. A. Lomov, ed., *Scientific-Technical Progress and the Revolution in Military Affairs*, Moscow: Military Publishing House, 1973; translated and published under the auspices of the US Air Force, Washington DC, 1974, p. 29.)
[31] Obviously a full-fledged military alliance, for example on the basis of the Lisbon force goals, would never have displayed similar political advantages. In fact its very political survivability might have been in jeopardy early in the game.
[32] For a fuller discussion of the instrumentalities of generalized threat perceptions see Uwe Nerlich, 'Continuity and Change: The Political Context of Western Europe's Defence' in Holst/Nerlich, *op. cit.* in note 11, pp. 24–9.

of political coherence, even though security interests and the scope for sharing common responsibilities in fact differed enormously among member states. Its military command structure was regarded as a kind of international regime of national contingents, although in reality NATO commands were essentially, in the words of a former commander of AAFCE (General Vogt), 'planning headquarters lacking full-scale operational staffs and survivable command and control facilities'. Military forces appeared to be tightly integrated but, except for air defence and scheduled nuclear strike programmes, this integration was largely symbolic. Military responses to actual threats were given essentially NATO-wide consideration so as to dampen adventurism and narrow the scope for sub-regional or other selective types of co-operation in favour of centralized control and apparent solidarity. But the dominance of US-controlled nuclear responses and their limited practicality in a wide variety of possible contingencies made it doubtful whether the only plausible response – an American one – would be forthcoming.

Obviously this political posture of the Alliance no longer serves its original purposes; nor is it going to survive politically or meet the kinds of threat which the West is increasingly facing. The Alliance will have to cope with a much wider range of threats.[33] It will have to operate in full recognition of the fact that it represents a coalition of independent nations who must be interdependent in their requirements for survival. Its military command structure will have to acquire more operational capabilities for a wide range of responses; preparations will have to increase for operational compatibility of coalition forces; possible responses have to be generated with a degree of flexibility which can meet specific crises of a NATO-wide, sub-regional or peripheral nature.

While nuclear technology in the past reinforced (and in fact enabled) what appeared to be the most desirable political posture of the Alliance, its subsequent continued and full exploitation was constrained for the same reasons. While 'stability' hardly displayed the kind of rationality which characterizes the inner working of the system, dominant beliefs about

what would destabilize the system nevertheless reflected recognized priorities.

New Technologies and Political Purpose
Today the Alliance has the potential ability to create a coalition posture which can deny Soviet offensive options short of a full-blown onslaught with deliberate nuclear strikes against Western Europe. Once again, new technologies would have an important part to play in the process. But the new posture would be the result not just of a utilization of new technologies but of a complex improvement effort involving major changes in force structure, strategy, tactics and equipment. And it would result not from high level political choices at a few junctures but from a lengthy process ranging over two or more legislative periods – though political choices would have to be made to keep up the momentum, and some major improvements could be achieved quite quickly.

Unlike Alliance practice in the past, political choices during the process cannot be construed in terms of alternative concepts of regional order of Atlantic systems, nor will any conceivable improvement programme actually produce new types of political relationships.[34] There is no way that NATO can regain its former role as the dominant Western foreign policy framework, and no change in NATO's military posture will restore some kind of unitary military super-structure – as was the case with theatre nuclear weapons until a few years ago. While NATO's nuclear system still affects its whole military posture, both because of its indispensability and the profound uncertainties which are associated with it, its capabilities are increasingly seen in terms of defence requirements, rather than nuclear deterrence, and operational needs, rather than nuclear control.[35] There will continue to be American dominance in NATO, but nuclear control will not again be the main vehicle, nor is there any escape from the fact that NATO's posture cannot be anything other than a coalition posture.

---

[33] For a more systematic description of the range of possible Soviet threats see Nerlich, *op. cit.* in note 32, pp. 29–36.

[34] See also Burt, *op. cit.* in note 5, p. 31.
[35] This results not only from the growing importance of conventional capabilities but also from the major shift in nuclear holdings from air to ground forces, particularly from scheduled strike programmes which bear a high degree of automaticity to organic weapons 'of opportunity'.

Despite the political utilities of military power in Europe, a more viable military posture for the Alliance could have important political purposes – notably in the context of a maturing Soviet military threat against Western Europe. It could prevent a deterioration of relations with the Soviet Union as influence grows more unbalanced. It could prevent a deterioration of Atlantic relations in terms of a fading strategic rationale for a continued American military engagement in Western Europe. And, possibly most important, a more viable military posture could have a stabilizing effect on Western Europe itself, by reducing its proneness to external pressure and producing a greater stability of political expectations. This would be favoured, it seems, not only by countries or political forces actively involved in NATO: notwithstanding their political preferences, Gaullists as well as the Italian Communist Party, Yugoslavia as well as Sweden, have an obvious interest in seeing Soviet military power checked by Allied capabilities. In fact it is increasingly recognized that political stability and economic well-being can be jeopardized in a variety of contingencies other than overt Soviet aggression against NATO. Unlike the nuclear posture of previous years, a coalition posture (such as may result from future improvements) could well enable control of this increasing range of possible contingencies.

Thus, once again in NATO history, new weapons technologies may profoundly appeal to a set of social values. It has been argued that the 'character of new weapons technology seems to be reinforcing tendencies towards a more fragmented and pluralistic international system'.[36] But as far as the Alliance is concerned this is not certain. If sustained improvement efforts succeed, the Alliance will indeed be more pluralistic, in terms of a greater capacity for selective co-operation and specific responses, but only on the basis of much increased allied co-operation on various levels, some NATO-wide, some concerned with functional selection, some sub-regional. On the other hand, if improvement efforts fail, the impact of new technologies will be at best altogether marginal: it would not suffice to preserve the international structures in the West which reflect basic social values of Western society.

Improvement efforts will not be uniform and definable in terms of shares of member states. Some will concern collective functions, for example some information-processing functions. Some will concern the nations committed to co-operation under the concept of integrated forward defence (i.e., the central region). Some will deal with the requirements for local resistance in order to allow for Allied reinforcements (in Norway for example). Some will indeed be needed to generate a capacity to project power into peripheral crises and prevent results which may impair Western Europe's security. In operational terms more independent or selective action will be required in a variety of circumstances. At the same time new interdependencies among Allies will flow from the application of new technologies, in the fields of information processing, electronic countermeasures, logistics, etc. Some will establish additional dependence on the United States, for example for information for terminal guidance for specific systems and missions.[37]

But while such dependencies may affect specific weapons choices (long-range cruise missiles with conventional warheads or non-American forces, for example), they will not determine the kind of co-operative relationships which will or will not develop within the Alliance. Rather, it will depend on the nature of emerging co-operative patterns within the Alliance whether or not new technologies are fully exploited.

Given the need for increased political as well as military flexibility within the Alliance, new technologies obviously seem as attractive as did nuclear technology in the 1950s. There is no way to predict what kind of Alliance posture will develop in the 1980s and 1990s, or in fact whether the Alliance will remain a condition of political stability and economic welfare for its members. If it does, it will have required more than efforts to improve standardization of equipment. If it does not, political geography is likely to change profoundly before the end of the century, new weapons technologies notwithstanding.

[36] Burt, op. cit., in note 5, p. 31.

[37] Moreover, large-scale modernization would obviously serve American industrial interests in reinforcing efforts towards increased two-way traffic, although one should also keep in mind that this would involve essentially the four Western nations, which together account for roughly 90 per cent of Western military R&D spending – the United States, Britain, France and West Germany.

Implications for Arms Control

RICHARD BURT

New technologies, while creating intriguing new options for Western military forces have also created some new, serious difficulties in existing institutions for East–West arms control. In this article the nature of these problems – and their implications for existing and future approaches to arms control – will be examined. The article will try essentially to determine whether it will be necessary to forgo the military advantages promised by the new technologies in order to preserve arms control or, alternatively, whether arms control should be adapted so that the new technologies can be widely exploited.

Controlling Military Innovation

There is a direct link between arms control and technological change, but the relationship is immensely complicated. Developments in the military 'state of the art' can be shown to have influenced the decisions of states over whether or not to go to war and have also conditioned the character of conflict if it occurred. Thus agreement to stop or slow down the development and deployment of new weapons has traditionally been understood to be a primary objective of formal arms-control negotiations. Yet the difficulties of halting, or even regulating, military innovation are formidable, and past efforts have rarely yielded positive results. At a time when technological innovation is nearly continuous, and the boundaries between military and civilian technology are almost non-existent, the capacity of states to agree on workable arrangements for putting an end to military innovation is particularly limited.[1] And even where this is possible, it is not always desirable. There are in fact three arguments that suggest that military innovation can sometimes be compatible with the objectives usually sought for arms control: strengthening deterrence, limiting war and saving money.

First, the impact of technological innovation on the propensity of states to go to war should not be viewed in isolation, but in the context of the overall military relationship that prevails between potential adversaries. While some innovation on the part of one of two evenly matched and technologically comparable adversaries might increase the chances of conflict, in a situation where one party enjoys advantages in manpower, equipment, numbers or geography, however, the ability of the other side to exploit technological advantages may be seen as a necessary means of maintaining an equilibrium in military capabilities. In reality – as the NATO–Warsaw Pact, Arab–Israeli and Sino–Soviet balances suggest – numerical military parity is the exception rather than the rule; qualitative advantages are exploited by many states as the most cost-effective means of compensating for quantitative deficiencies. In the specific case of the European balance US Secretary of Defense Harold Brown recently noted: 'We need not match the enemy tank for tank. If properly managed, new techniques for target acquisition, delivery systems, and precision guidance should make our task of defence easier.'[2]

Second, technological innovation does not necessarily weaken deterrence nor always make

[1] See Hedley Bull's arguments in 'The Problem of Continuous Innovation', Chapter 12, *The Control of the Arms Race* (London: Weidenfeld, 1961).

[2] *Statement by Defense Secretary Harold Brown on Long-Term Program for NATO*, delivered before the Manpower and Personnel Subcommittee of the Senate Armed Services Committee, 3 August 1977 (United States Information Service).

war more destructive. The deployment of less vulnerable weapons can lessen the incentives to mount a surprise attack: the introduction of ballistic missile submarines in the 1960s, for example, was seen by many to bolster strategic stability between the super-powers. The deployment of more reliable and discriminate weapons can also reduce the destructiveness of warfare – more accurate munitions delivery, for instance, enabled the United States Air Force progressively to reduce collateral damage caused by bombing during the course of the Vietnam war. With the advent of new munitions and long-range precision-guided delivery vehicles, like cruise missiles, the possibility that conventional weapons might be used against targets that in the past were thought to require nuclear warheads seems an instance where technological innovation is consonant with a widely shared arms-control objective: reducing wartime pressures to resort to the use of nuclear weapons.

Third, while there is general agreement that arms races between states tend to generate an unhealthy momentum of their own and thus reinforce the political differences that first inspire military competition, it has also been noted that some arms races are more dangerous than others. Military competition characterized by rapid equipment modernization – so-called 'qualitative arms races' – seems on the surface to be especially risky because of the potentially dramatic impact that new weapons can have on military balances. But by creating new uncertainties the introduction of new weapons technologies makes calculations on the performance of forces more difficult, and can thus serve to inhibit a would-be aggressor from confidently going to war. Furthermore, as Samuel Huntington noted years ago, qualitative arms races, because they force rivals periodically to 'start from scratch' in the deployment of new systems, have less frequently led to conflict than straight competition in levels of existing arms.[3] In this vein it has been suggested that NATO's deployment of a new generation of anti-armour weapons may force the Soviet army to undertake some extensive and time-consuming changes in tactics and force design that could lessen the likelihood of conflict in Europe during the next decade.[4]

This is not to argue that any effort to control technological innovation is likely to be unworkable or undesirable. There can be little doubt that military innovation can sometimes have an unfavourable effect on international security; but this is not always the case. The new technologies of precision delivery and target discrimination presently entering NATO inventories promise to have a positive impact on East–West deterrence and defence. In the abstract the most effective approach to controlling military innovation is one that is able to discriminate between favourable and unfavourable weapons developments. Qualitative arms-control, in other words, must be selective: while some developments should be stopped, others need to be protected or even encouraged.

But if technological change is a fitting *subject* for arms-control negotiations to pursue, it can also be a *threat* to the continuity of negotiations. Arms-control proposals, as well as entire negotiating processes, can be made irrelevant by new weapons technologies: more powerful new weapons can change the 'unit of account' used by arms controllers in negotiating over force balances; longer-range weapons can make geographical assumptions no longer tenable; more flexible systems can threaten arrangements based on limiting the performance of specified military missions; and smaller, more mobile, weapons can complicate the task of verification. If new systems that threaten arms control are also judged to be inimical to deterring war or limiting damage in the event of war, then negotiators should encounter little trouble in stopping their deployment. If, on the other hand, certain new systems are judged to enhance military stability, then governments must face the difficult choice between jeopardizing current negotiations through technological innovation and forgoing the military benefits of new technologies in order to sustain negotiations. Because arms-control negotiations are often

---

[3] 'Arms Races: Pre-requisites and Results' in Carl Friedrich and Seymour E. Harris, *Public Policy* (Graduate School of Public Administration, Harvard University, 1958).

[4] Edward Atkeson has argued that the Soviet army faces an overwhelming set of problems in adapting to new anti-tank technology. (See 'Is the Soviet Army Obsolete?', *Army*, May 1974.) Phillip Karber, on the other hand, has argued that this process of adjustment is already well under way and presents NATO with a new set of tactical challenges. (See 'The Soviet Anti-Tank Debate', *Survival*, May/June 1976.)

assigned economic objectives and important political roles, as well as tackling military problems, this choice is not easy to make. However, new technologies do not always threaten existing negotiations and – of more importance – arms-control negotiations can be designed to accommodate military innovation. If arms control is to be effective, negotiations must not only be able to discriminate between new technologies; they must also be able to adapt to technological change.

Discrimination and Adaptation: Past Lessons

How are criteria arrived at for distinguishing between weapons? Because a primary aim of arms control is to make military aggression more difficult, negotiators have traditionally sought arrangements in which the defensive capabilities of states would be strengthened while offensive capabilities were curtailed. But this is no simple task.

That this is so was illustrated by the unsuccessful effort of the League of Nations during the inter-war period to limit the deployment of 'aggressive' weapons. Participants in the process quickly learned the futility of trying to establish a universal system for classifying 'offensive' and 'defensive' weapons. Most weapons which appeared offensive could be used in defensive roles, and *vice versa*. As a result the definitions put forward by governments were subjective judgments based on national interest.[5] Larger maritime powers such as Britain viewed large surface warships as a means of protecting global sea lines of communication and thus insisted that warships were 'defensive' in character; weaker coastal states such as Greece, on the other hand, saw the power of the major navies as constituting an 'offensive threat'. On land, continental powers like France argued that the ability to mobilize large numbers of reserves quickly was an essential aspect of defence, while British commentators noted that a rapid mobilization capability could be exploited for surprise offensives. France also objected to efforts by the Soviet Union and Germany, among others, to place weight restrictions on tanks, arguing instead that they could make as impor-

tant a contribution to the defence as the offence. These differences were reflected in much of the debate that surrounded the League's efforts. While strategists of the so-called 'mechanical school' (Liddell Hart for example) generally supported the idea of limiting weapons like tanks and heavy-payload aircraft that in their view would favour the attacker, others (including J. F. C. Fuller) noted that these same weapons, by emphasizing manoeuvre rather than firepower, held out the promise of reducing much of the carnage associated with immobile trench warfare. Fuller and his colleagues further argued that distinctions made by disarmament experts between 'defensive' and 'offensive' weapons were, in reality, differences only in weapon size, destructiveness and range.

The League discussions, which culminated in the abortive World Disarmament Conference of 1932–3, did not only underline the difficulties of discrimination. Most of the debates that took place during this period failed to anticipate how new technology would be exploited in World War II and so emphasized also the problem of adaptation. Numerous instances can be cited of the failure of governments during these talks to understand the military impact of new developments. In naval arms-control discussions, for example, Britain rejected Japanese efforts to limit aircraft carrier deployment because the Royal Navy saw the carrier useful only as a reconnaissance arm of the fleet. Similarly, one of the more striking developments of World War II was to be the German exploitation of aircraft for close air support of the army: working in conjunction with tank forces aircraft were to become a vital complement to the armoured *Blitzkrieg*. But, as Kemp has recorded, the fact that separate League commissions dealt with ground, naval and air forces in isolation made it practically impossible for negotiators to deal with the growing integration of military activity in different mediums.[6] (It should be

[5] Geoffrey Kemp, *Classification of Weapons Systems and Force Designs in Less Developed Country Environments: Implications for Arms Transfer Policies* (Center for International Studies, MIT, 1970), pp. 5–20.

[6] Germany's particular sensitivity to the impact of new technologies during the inter-war period was partly caused by the arms-control regime forced upon her in the Treaty of Versailles. Stripped of most of its war-making capability after World War I, the German military establishment was in effect freed from the 'drag' of an outdated inventory of weapons and was forced to consider radical new ideas. The Versailles restrictions themselves contributed to German military innovation. The development of new air defence guns and smaller close support

noted that the inability of negotiators to perceive the implications of combined-arms operations was a direct product of the unwillingness of most military elites during this period to exploit opportunities for co-operation among the service arms.)

However, the most telling example of the difficulty of adapting arms control to a new generation of weapons technology comes from the one 'successful' effort at limiting arms during the inter-war period – the 1922 and 1930 Washington and London Naval Treaties. These agreements (which, incidentally, did not provide for procedures of verification) placed a number of different restrictions on naval forces, including overall tonnage limits, ceilings on different types of warships, limits on the size of guns and restrictions on basing. Unlike the League discussions, those in the naval arena were not hampered by many of the subjective considerations of national interest that arose in arms-control efforts on the land and in the air. This, as Philip Noel Baker argued in 1926, was because naval warfare seemed a far less complicated business to analyse: 'Naval disarmament is, in itself, a simpler technical problem than the disarmament of land or air forces – simpler, because, in naval armaments, the doctrine of the "dominant factor" comes so near to being true that a treaty which limits warships and the guns they carry, neglecting all other factors of naval strength, will virtually solve the problem.'[7] In less than a decade, of course, the maturing of submarine and naval air technologies had already made the 'dominant factors' of ship size and gun calibre obsolete, and with them the naval treaties of 1922 and 1930. The rising naval ambitions of Germany and Japan during this period fostered the development of new systems and new techniques which created negotiating problems that were not anticipated in the 1920s.

But perhaps the most interesting aspect of naval negotiations during the mid-1930s was the problem that Britian and the United States had in reconciling the naval 'central balance' between them established by the Washington Treaty with their changing theatre requirements resulting from German and Japanese naval developments. Britain, sensitive to German naval rearmament, and the United States, reacting to Japanese developments, found themselves with very different naval building requirements, and thus increasingly at odds over new formulae to institutionalize their naval parity.[8] The result was the replacement of the relatively simple 1922 and 1930 agreements with a complicated set of multilateral and bilateral agreements that finally collapsed under their own weight towards the end of the decade.

The Nuclear Era: New Criteria for Arms Control

The problems created by new technologies in the conduct of East–West arms control in the nuclear era bear little superficial resemblance to the difficulties which hampered negotiations in the inter-war years. Yet a closer examination reveals some basic similarities between the definitional and structural challenges to arms control raised by military innovation during the two periods. However, to appreciate these similarities it is necessary first to recognize the important impact that nuclear weapons had on arms-control thinking in the post-war era.

Because of their destructive power nuclear weapons led to the elaboration in the West of strategies of deterrence which essentially institutionalized the role of the offence in military strategy and later at the Strategic Arms Limitations Talks (SALT) between the two nuclear super-powers. As a result the problem of distinguishing between 'offensive' and 'defensive'

---

aircraft like the *Stuka*, for example, resulted from restrictions placed on German development of artillery and high-payload bombers. See Eric Morris *et al.*, *Weapons & Warfare of the 20th Century* (London: Octopus Books, 1976), pp. 190–194. The tendency of arms control often to act as spur to military innovation is a phenomenon that of course has not gone unnoticed in recent years. The US cruise missile has been widely described as an unanticipated by-product of limits placed on US–Soviet ballistic missiles in 1972.
[7] P. J. Noel Baker, *Disarmament* (London: The Hogarth Press, 1926), p. 174.

[8] By 1934 Britain, concerned over German naval rearmament, was seeking an arrangement that would allow her higher cruiser levels when the London Treaty expired in 1936. The United States, worried over Japanese demands for naval parity, sought reductions in a follow-on agreement and was shocked by the British proposal for higher ceilings. This marked the turning point of inter-naval arms control. British efforts to submerge these differences – in the context of new proposals designed to limit qualitative developments rather than ship tonnage – failed. See John Barton, *When Arms Control Declines: Possible Lessons from the 1930s* (unpublished paper).

weapons became irrelevant and as with naval disarmament in the 1920s, the task confronting arms controllers was simplified by the emergence of a new 'dominant factor' – nuclear firepower – that seemed to make differences between the United States and the Soviet Union in tactics, geography, population and resources seem unimportant. While theoretical debates over the advisability of closing off options to mount a strategic defence continued, there emerged a general consensus (at least in the West) that the creation and maintenance of a situation of mutual vulnerability to strategic attack was the primary means of inhibiting East–West military conflict. 'Deterrent stability' became the new criterion for strategic arms limitation. This understanding was reflected in the 1972 SALT agreements which restricted the deployment of ballistic missile defences while allowing both sides to expand and modernize their offensive missile forces.

The nuclear build-up undertaken by the two super-powers in the post-war era radically altered the place of conventional weapons in arms-control thinking. The critical link between conventional conflict and nuclear escalation meant that conventional arms control had to be tailored to the perceived requirements of strategic stability. Warsaw Pact conventional military preponderance, together with the terrible risks of escalation implicit in strategies of nuclear deterrence, made the expansion and modernization of conventional capabilities by the West a necessity, and one not inconsistent with stable deterrence. As advocates of a 'flexible response' capability for NATO argued during the 1960s, an improved conventional posture in Western Europe would not only reduce the likelihood that local conflicts might quickly move to general nuclear war but, in providing governments with greater flexibility in the event of conflict, a stalwart conventional defence would also enhance the credibility of the deterrent threat. As a result the relative improvement of NATO's theatre capabilities was judged in the West to be an important arms-control objective in itself.

This objective placed limits on what arms control in Europe could achieve. The Soviet effort in the 1950s to make Europe into a nuclear-free zone was undesirable because it would have stripped away the nuclear deterrent to regional conflict – as to a lesser degree would the more recent Warsaw Pact proposal to ban the first use of nuclear weapons. Eastern proposals to 'freeze' the conventional balance in Europe were also seen to be undesirable, but for a very different reason: limits placed on NATO conventional force improvement would have recognized formally Soviet conventional superiority and made the Alliance *too* dependent on the nuclear deterrent. The concern for enhancing (or at least preserving) NATO's conventional posture therefore became the dominant aim of the West in pursuing Mutual and Balanced Force Reductions (MBFR) with the Warsaw Pact at the Vienna talks in the 1970s. The Western desire to improve NATO capabilities *vis-à-vis* the Warsaw Pact was reflected in what Western governments sought in an agreement – parity in ground force numbers in the centre region of Europe. But this desire was perhaps more strongly reflected in what Western governments did *not* seek from MBFR – limits on equipment numbers or constraints on equipment modernization which might have interfered with efforts to bolster NATO's theatre defences.

Thus in the early 1970s SALT and MBFR provided a framework for East–West arms control within which the West could pursue the twin objectives of inhibiting the outbreak of war and limiting its consequences if it occurred: SALT became a forum for the United States to perfect strategic deterrence, while MBFR became a forum for the Alliance to enhance its theatre defences. This two-tier structure meant that in military terms there was no inconsistency between the exercise of technological restraint by the super-powers on the strategic level and the exploitation of new technologies by the United States and her allies in the theatre. In political terms it meant that there was no inconsistency between consolidating super-power strategic relations at SALT and maintaining the cohesion of the Alliance at MBFR.

While conceptually elegant, this arms-control framework never quite corresponded to reality. The 'division of labour' represented by SALT and MBFR did not correspond neatly to a nuclear/conventional distinction because both NATO and the Warsaw Pact deployed a variety of shorter-range, and generally smaller yield, 'tactical' nuclear weapons in the European theatre. Nor was the strategic/theatre distinction erected by SALT–MBFR entirely accurate. Because SALT was a bilateral forum the place of the strategic forces deployed by Britain and France was ambiguous. So too was the status of Soviet intermediate-range missiles (IRBM) and bombers: while these systems could threaten Western Europe with strategic attack they did not pose a threat to the United States. Finally, there were US forward-based systems (FBS) in Europe – land and carrier-based strike aircraft – which were assigned nuclear and conventional theatre strike missions but in theory also possessed the ability to carry out strategic strikes against the Soviet Union.

Taken together these different categories of weapons constituted a 'grey area' in East–West arms control that raised a host of potential problems for the United States and her allies. As we have seen, a fundamental assumption underlying the Western willingness to enter into the two sets of negotiations was that attempts to stabilize the US–Soviet strategic balance would not come at the expense of improvements to NATO's theatre capabilities. Yet the prospect that American dual-capable systems in Europe might be limited at SALT (while at the same time Soviet intermediate-range systems were left untouched) raised serious questions over whether this assumption was justified. However, in the early years of both SALT and MBFR Western governments were able in practice to avoid the sensitive questions raised by the 'grey area'. At SALT the Soviet Union did make a bid to limit Alliance theatre capabilities by seeking direct limits on US forward-based systems and an indirect ceiling on French and British nuclear forces. However, the United States (under strong pressure from her European allies) resisted these Soviet efforts to tamper with Alliance defences, and in 1972 the super-powers agreed to a five-year arrangement under which only inter-continental ballistic missiles (ICBM) and submarine-launched ballistic missiles (SLBM) – so-called 'central' strategic systems – were placed under ceilings at SALT. In the guidelines for a new ten-year SALT agreement agreed to at Vladivostok in November 1974 the United States was again successful in keeping theatre-based systems outside the boundaries of agreement. At MBFR Western negotiators also resisted Soviet pressure to discuss limitations on equipment numbers, particularly aircraft and nuclear warheads, and insisted instead that the negotiations confine themselves to working out a formula for parity in ground force numbers.

New Technologies and the 'Grey Area'

By the end of 1975, however, it grew increasingly obvious that the Alliance could not pursue arms-control agreements while maintaining complete flexibility in theatre force modernization. Frustrated over the lack of progress at the Vienna talks, NATO negotiators (at US instigation) proposed that troop reductions be tied to a scheme under which American nuclear warheads and delivery vehicles in the centre region would be reduced in return for cuts in Soviet armour. Because Soviet tanks made up the most troubling element of the Warsaw Pact threat this proposal seemed a sensible one. Yet, as we will see below, its implications for NATO's ability to modernize its theatre nuclear stockpile as well as delivery capabilities, for conventional as well as nuclear munitions, were not widely appreciated.

Far more important than NATO's nuclear offer at MBFR, however, was the US and Soviet development and – in certain cases – initial deployment of a new generation of multi-role missiles and aircraft. Although each of these systems incorporated different technologies their general effect was the same: they increased the military and political significance of the 'grey area' described above. Consequently, the artificial boundaries dividing 'strategic' and 'theatre' military concerns were weakened further. At SALT, negotiations soon became dominated by arguments over what was, and was not, a 'strategic' weapon. At Vladivostok the two sides had agreed to limit long-range bombers in a new accord, and afterwards the United States pushed for the inclusion of the new Soviet variable-geometry *Backfire* bomber under the ceilings because, under certain assumptions, it could threaten targets in the United States. The Soviet Union fiercely resisted this move, arguing that the bomber was not intended for inter-continental-range missions but for naval missions and theatre roles in Europe and Asia. A potentially similar problem emerged somewhat later when the Soviet Union moved to deploy a new mobile IRBM, the SS-20: although the missile, when equipped with multiple warheads, did not appear to have the necessary range to threaten US targets, it was possible that equipped with a smaller warhead or an additional booster stage (transforming it into an SS-16 ICBM) the SS-20 could become a 'strategic' weapon.

But the most daunting problem of definition was raised by the American development of a new family of highly efficient precision-guided aerodynamic drones – cruise missiles. Launched from the air, ground, on or under the sea the cruise missiles under development in the United States were highly 'elastic' weapons. Armed with nuclear or a new class of specialized conventional munitions, and equipped with various guidance packages, cruise missiles appeared capable of performing a wide variety of roles, ranging from long-range anti-shipping missions to deep-penetration strikes against heavily-defended rear-area targets. Equipped only with sensory devices or jammers cruise missiles even promised to perform surveillance and electronic-warfare roles. In the performance of these tasks cruise missiles thus offered military advantages that seemed entirely consistent with Western arms-control objectives in Europe: a more dispersed and more survivable land and sea-based theatre strike capability; a more reliable and cheaper means of penetrating to enemy targets; the ability to reduce unwanted collateral damage in weapons delivery; and, perhaps most interesting, the opportunity to use conventional munitions in roles previously assigned to nuclear weapons. Of course the central problem was that, configured differently, the cruise missile could also be used for strategic bombardment, and the Soviet Union therefore attached tremendous importance to including it in a new SALT agreement – restricting its range, its deployment aboard various launchers and its development in certain modes.

Given the system's potential as a strategic weapon, the Soviet Union's campaign for cruise missile limitations at SALT was understandable. But if in theory it was possible to distinguish between different versions of the cruise missile, the enormous problems of policing a SALT agreement that included cruise missiles meant in practice that restrictions placed on 'strategic' versions would inevitably hamper their exploitation for military missions in and around Europe. Thus the effect of the cruise missile problem at SALT was to re-introduce the FBS issue into the talks in a new and far more pronounced manner. If the United States agreed to limit cruise missiles in the bilateral negotiating context of SALT she would probably have to pass up the opportunity to modernize her theatre delivery capabilities, and would thus be taking a decision that would affect the defence posture of the Alliance as a whole. Moreover, while cruise missile controls at SALT would only directly limit US options, non-circumvention provisions or restrictions on technology transfer could also act to limit options for US allies. With the Soviet Union in the process of modernizing her own 'Eurostrategic' capabilities with the *Backfire* and the SS-20, a decision by the United States to accept major restrictions on cruise missiles would almost certainly arouse serious tensions within the Alliance. This would be particularly true if outcomes at SALT interacted in an unforeseen way with proposals at MBFR to limit US aircraft and missiles in exchange for Soviet tank reductions. As mentioned above an important question that would have to be addressed in framing such a deal at MBFR is how it would affect future US and European delivery options in Central Europe. It would be important, of course, that this be assessed by NATO as a whole. But a decision taken at super-power level to restrict cruise missile deployment could serve to pre-empt Alliance consideration of the problem at MBFR. In a variety of different respects, then, the new generation of technology embodied in the cruise missile has forced the United States and her allies to confront the difficult choice between achieving US–Soviet strategic stability and NATO–Warsaw Pact theatre stability – a choice the existing framework for East–West arms-control had been earlier designed to avoid.

Thus, the problems that hampered East–West negotiations during 1975–77 are not very different, in the abstract, from the difficulties that marked arms-control efforts during the inter-war period. The inability of negotiators at SALT to agree on what weapons fit into the 'strategic' category, for example, is analogous to the difficulties of definition encountered by League of Nations disarmament experts in identifying 'aggressive' weapons. Negotiators in both sets of talks had to adjust painfully to the fact that new weapons, together with new concepts for their employment, made it increasingly difficult to classify weapons in terms of their dominant military role. Another problem that also surfaced in the League talks – the failure to recognize that new developments had made efforts to compartmentalize negotiations covering land, air and naval forces obsolete – corresponds to the contemporary problem of identifying the complicated linkages between SALT and MBFR. However, it is the collapse of naval arms control during the mid-1930s that contains some of the most important parallels to the existing situation. The inability of the two 'naval super-powers' of the period – the United States and Britain – to stabilize their own naval relationship while concurrently maintaining the flexibility to react to changing regional requirements is the core problem that the United States, in terms of the European theatre, and the Soviet Union, in terms of her relationship with China, face at SALT.

Technological Restraint versus Structural Change

If East–West arms control is not to go the way of inter-war disarmament attempts, the means will have to be found to make SALT and MBFR more responsive to technological change. The problems created by the new generation of 'elastic' military technology will not be solved, as some have argued, by adopting a general policy of 'technological restraint'. The difficulty with technological restraint is not simply that it is difficult to enforce but that, in the case of most of the systems now under development, it is also undesirable. If they are properly incorporated into NATO force structures the technologies associated with the 'PGM revolution' will strengthen conventional defences and bolster nuclear deterrence. Thus it is fallacious to argue that developments like the cruise missile pose a fundamental threat to East–West military stability; the problem is that they threaten the existing institutions of East–West arms control. Institutional adaptation, rather than technological restraint, is therefore the most important priority for East–West arms control at the present time.

But what sort of adaptation is necessary? To answer this question it is essential to recognize that military innovation has made it no longer possible, for purposes of negotiation, to dissociate the US–Soviet strategic balance from the NATO–Warsaw Pact balance in Europe. This means that SALT and MBFR will somehow have to be reorganized to manage the growing interdependence between global and regional, nuclear and conventional components of the East–West military relationship. In theory there are a variety of ways this might be attempted. The geographical boundaries of MBFR might be extended so that the 'grey area' could be covered in a force-reductions agreement. Alternatively, SALT and MBFR could be merged into a 'comprehensive' forum for East–West arms control. Still another option would be to deal with the 'grey area' in a new forum for 'regional' nuclear systems. Superficially appealing as any one of these schemes might appear, the political and military problems of formally restructuring arms control along any of these lines should not be underestimated. The super-powers, for a start, can be expected to resist strongly any effort to alter bilateralism at SALT; correspondingly, the Western Europeans – particularly France – are equally reticent about becoming participants in an arms-control process which would surely reduce their nuclear autonomy. In addition to this, as long as there is the slightest chance of success at SALT or MBFR governments are unlikely to entertain seriously any scheme that would essentially force the negotiations to begin again from scratch. Like weapons projects, arms-control institutions acquire their own bureaucratic constituencies which can become psychologically wedded to existing negotiating processes.

If the formal restructuring of East–West arms control is unrealistic, a more informal method might produce results. Because the 'grey area' has primarily hampered negotiations at SALT there is a strong case for making a virtue out of the growing necessity for the talks to focus on issues that directly affect European security. The two super-powers could then discuss proposals at SALT that limited 'Eurostrategic' systems such as cruise missiles, medium-range aircraft and IRBM as well as 'central' systems like ICBM, SLBM and heavy bombers. The interested parties in Western Europe would not formally participate in the super-power dialogue but they would be offered the opportunity to participate fully with the United States in framing proposals and responses to Soviet initiatives. The aim would be to establish an Alliance position at SALT, to provide the Europeans with every means of influencing the outcome of the talks, short of actually sitting at the negotiating table. SALT, in other words, would remain a bilateral enterprise in form only.

Although this approach would not necessitate a formal restructuring of SALT, it would require some substantial changes in the way the United States, Western Europe and the Soviet Union approach the talks. In order to minimize the Alliance discord that would arise from limiting FBS or cruise missiles at SALT, the United States would have to give up her special channel of communication with the Soviet Union in the full knowledge that widening the scope of the negotiations to include theatre-based systems, and giving the Europeans the chance to influence negotiating policy, would complicate the task of formulating proposals and obtaining agreements. The Europeans, who have strongly resisted the idea of letting SALT tamper with Alliance defence arrangements, would have to pay this price in order to gain semi-admission to the talks and the opportunity to limit Soviet Eurostrategic forces for the first time. For the Soviet Union the price for limiting Western FBS would be the acceptance of limits on her own theatre options.

If SALT were informally 'multilateralized' along the lines suggested above, some of the tensions that have hampered recent negotiations might quickly disappear. But many would still remain. Most important, the formulation of a common Alliance position at SALT would still not ease the problem of reconciling the conflicting pressures of super-power consolidation and Alliance cohesion. However, by forcing governments to review both the global and the regional implications of various proposals, the trade-offs between consolidating US–Soviet strategic relations and protecting theatre capabilities would be able to be examined in a comprehensive fashion. Put more simply, there may indeed be a strong case for curbing cruise missile deployment in order to obtain a new SALT agreement, but until the military implications of this step are fully thrashed out within the Alliance as a whole the political costs of taking it will be high.

If a case can be made for enlarging the scope of the SALT exercise, just the reverse is true for MBFR. The NATO attempt to break the deadlock in Vienna by introducing nuclear warheads and – more important – delivery vehicles into the negotiations has already created potential jurisdictional problems with SALT. If, as seems inevitable, the super-power dialogue becomes more deeply concerned with theatre systems, the difficulties of co-ordinating negotiations at MBFR

and SALT will only worsen. Hence the temptation to 'sweeten' proposals for manpower reductions by offering additional limits on Western aircraft and tactical missiles should be resisted. In fact there is a strong argument for avoiding limitations on military equipment in Central Europe altogether. As Steven Canby has argued, the West has sought through negotiation at Vienna what it should have long ago achieved unilaterally – a credible conventional defence.[9] With a new generation of battlefield anti-armour weapons, improved air defences and target surveillance and engagement technologies, NATO – if it undertakes the necessary reforms – should be capable of coping with the Warsaw Pact tank threat. On the other hand, attempts to cope with the threat at MBFR by limiting equipment will not only hinder NATO modernization but would also forestall the structural changes that the Alliance so badly needs to undertake.

But parity in ground-force numbers – NATO's original goal in the talks – is also a problematic negotiating objective. The growing emphasis in Soviet force structure and doctrine on conventional operations using highly ready, forward-deployed shock forces, designed to strike before NATO defences are in place, presents a different military problem to that perceived by the West when the Vienna talks got under way. It is a problem that some argue is a direct result of NATO's interest in new anti-armour technology and, as Phillip Karber has noted, would be little affected by reductions in aggregate manpower or even equipment numbers.[10] If MBFR is to address the new short-warning attack threat, negotiators will have to worry less about overall numbers and more about specific military activities and dispositions. Johan Jørgen Holst and Karen Alette Melander have recently suggested that confidence-building measures (CBM) that would rule out surprise-attack options are one possible

[9] See Steven Canby, *MBFR: A Military Perspective of its Underpinnings* (Paper prepared for the Conference on 'The Changing Conditions of European Security', Aspen Institute, Berlin, 26–29 June 1977).
[10] Karber maintains that in achieving surprise, 'Warsaw Pact commanders would not need quantitative superiority to conduct prolonged attrition of NATO's defences. Instead, they could commit large armoured formations for high-speed envelopment and flanking action into the gaps in NATO's unprepared defences.' *Evolution of the Central European Military Balance* (BDM Corporation, 14 June 1977), p. 13.

answer.[11] In curtailing the 'shadow' rather than the 'substance' of military power in Europe CBM seem especially appropriate in an era when reductions in themselves will not necessarily lead to greater regional stability. Holst and Melander call for a new emphasis on CBM in the Vienna negotiations ('Associated Measures' in MBFR parlance) and also an effort to integrate NATO–Warsaw Pact understandings over troop dispositions, movements and exercises in a strengthened and broadened all-European CBM system that would be fashioned at the Conference on Security and Co-operation in Europe (CSCE). Although technology is pushing MBFR closer to SALT there seems to be a strong case for steering the Vienna talks towards CSCE – where negotiating outcomes are more likely to be complementary than contradictory.

More generally, the West both at SALT and MBFR should be wary of asking too much from arms control in a period of rapid technological change. If the arguments presented here are correct, the existing negotiations will have to undergo some important changes if arms control is to survive into the 1980s. Yet at the very time when arms control seems to be in the greatest trouble, it has become fashionable to insist that the aims of the talks should become more ambitious. At the best of times many of the objectives now sought by arms controllers would create difficult negotiating problems. At present proposals for 'deep cuts' in strategic forces, proportional reductions in equipment levels in Europe, restrictions on weapons testing or efforts to reach a 'consensus' on military doctrine will only complicate the problem of adapting East–West negotiations to a new technological era. Attractive as some of these ideas appear, there is a pressing need for Western governments – especially the new one in Washington – to sort out their priorities for arms control. The Carter Administration's attempt during 1977 to get the Soviet Union to accept some radically new ideas at SALT was probably premature. Before SALT or MBFR are assigned new tasks it will first be necessary to recognize that technology is rapidly making many of the assumptions that underlie the existing talks obsolete. Unless these assumptions are revised, and the structure of East–West negotiations and the process of intra-Alliance consultation correspondingly change, the future of arms control will be bleak.

---

[11] Johan Jørgen Holst and Karen Alette Melander, 'European Security and Confidence-Building Measures', *Survival*, July/August 1977; 'Surprise Attack', *NATO Review*, August 1977.

New Weapons Technology and the Offence/Defence Balance

ERIK KLIPPENBERG

In Europe the offence/defence balance depends on both conventional and nuclear capabilities and on the subtle interaction between the two. Significant innovations in nuclear weapons technology and several aspects of new conventional weapons technology could affect both. Changes in either technology could sway the balance. Although a somewhat factitious delimitation, nuclear weapons technology and operations are beyond the scope of this paper.

The nature of new conventional weapons technology is such that it will be exploited for both offensive and defensive purposes. In combat, both the aggressor and the defender will engage in offensive and defensive operations. In spite of limitations imposed by weather, terrain, etc., the potential consequences of new weapons technology for either are compelling and will probably lead to the development of new tactical options for offensive and defensive operations. The extent to which new weapons technology can be exploited could, however, be restricted by human physical endurance and mental capacity. The quantity of new-technology weapons in the forces would obviously depend on their cost and the defence budgets available. In Europe the nature and quality of civilian infrastructure would influence the outcome of military operations. The dynamics of the transformation of war potentials into combat-ready forces in the theatre would also affect the offence/defence balance at the conventional level.

As far as is known, no analysis has yet been undertaken of the broad range of problems which bear upon the implications of new conventional weapons technology to the offence/ defence balance. Only parts of the problem have been analysed. However, even if comprehensive analyses were available and a consistent under- standing of the probable consequences of rational application of new weapons technology had been developed, it is more probable than not that the real future would look different. The very war we strive to avoid might well be fought before the implications of new weapons technology are fully understood and accepted.

The aim of this paper is, therefore, neither to draw conclusions nor make predictions about the impact of new weapons technology on the offence/defence balance, but rather to identify important aspects of the problem and discuss their nature and potential consequences. The first assumption is that both sides have about equal access to new-technology weapons. This does not imply identical material in the same quantities, but rather the same technological state of the art and about equal emphasis on weapons and equipment in the forces. On the same assumption, the paper endeavours to identify those elements of operations in which technology might favour offence or defence and discusses factors which might be decisive. Since a definite technological lead would probably sway the balance in favour of that side, the final examination is of the factors which might affect NATO's ability to take advantage of technology in order to maintain a credible deterrence.

Basic and New Technologies

The complexity of military operations is such that any attempt to isolate and interrelate the main elements is likely to overlook aspects which could be important. In the combat zone, the commander's two basic options for influencing the outcome of a military confrontation are:

(i) to use manoeuvre to attain a winning concentration of forces at the actual point of combat or to deprive the enemy of any opportunity to attack one's own forces;

(ii) to use fire-power to inflict losses on opposing forces.

Tactical mobility is a major factor in commanders' ability to manoeuvre forces in the combat zone in order to achieve a winning concentration of forces in actual combat. The quality of tactical reconnaissance and the use made of information about enemy strength and deployment are also important to timely and successful manoeuvring of forces. The availability of combat-ready forces in the combat zone depends on the ability of commanders at higher levels to exploit reserves and support in the theatre. Timely transformation of national war potentials into strategic reserves and then theatre-level reserves and support will similarly hinge on the ability of military and political leaders to interpret strategic intelligence and reach decisions on strategic mobility, and on enemy interference.

This should not be allowed to leave the impression that all forces will end up in mutual annihilation. Many battles have been won through competent manoeuvring of forces and without infliction of high losses. Unless the density and effectiveness of fire in future wars completely outweighs advances in mobility, manoeuvres could be equally decisive in future battles.

Before discussing the potential impacts on the offence/defence balance, the characteristics of new weapons technology will be reviewed briefly and the possibility that new technology might, in certain respects, change the general nature of conventional warfare will be examined.

The Combat Zone

The impressive accuracy of new weapons systems hinges on some form of terminal guidance. Advances in electronic technology have made feasible the design of small and light TV, laser, infra-red (IR) and radar seekers and other terminal guidance systems compatible even with quite small weapons. Weapons so designed will have remarkable hit probabilities against point targets and, given target data, the potential for inflicting losses at startling rates. However, successful engagements require detection and acquisition of the target and, furthermore, that the target remains visible to the guidance system until the weapon reaches the target.

In Europe, moving targets taking advantage of terrain formations, vegetation and man-made structures reduce significantly the periods over which they are exposed to detection and tracking by weapon systems. For instance, in the hilly southern parts of Central Europe, the probability is about 0·7 that a tank moving at 15 km/hour at a range of 2,000 m is still visible to the anti-tank gunner when the weapon reaches the target area. This assumes a 10-second reaction time for the gunner and 10-second time of flight for the weapon. On the North German plains the probability would be only 0·4. Increased automation of acquisition and control may reduce delays somewhat, but weapon effectiveness will still be diminished by limited intervisibility and delays.

New electro-optical sensors, particularly when carried aloft by aircraft or remotely piloted vehicles (RPV), will increase the capacity of tactical reconnaissance systems to detect and locate even stationary and partially concealed targets day and night. However, weather in Central Europe could often reduce the usefulness of airborne electro-optical sensors. Depending on the season, from three to eight days of the month have more than 50 per cent cloud cover below 1,000 ft. Improved airborne radars with detection ranges of several tens of kilometres against moving and exposed targets would improve all-weather reconnaissance, but could hardly be used for target acquisition. Enemy ground-to-air weapons will also impair airborne surveillance operations.

In spite of several restricting factors, the overall capacity of precision-guided weapons to destroy targets will be high. New area weapons of the cluster and fuel–air explosive types will increase the effect of fire against soft targets. In future combat, therefore, the loss rates for personnel and weapon systems could well be tellingly higher than before.

Up to now night combat has largely had the character of static weapons employment in defence. Increased range and capacity of passive electro-optical sensors will give tanks, mechanized infantry and attack helicopters the capacity to engage and manoeuvre at night. Integrated arms teams will have the capability to fight at night as they can in the day.

Turning specifically to manoeuvring, the helicopter has the capacity to increase tactical mobility considerably. The attack helicopter with new fire control, rockets, high firing-rate cannons, and precision-guided weapons will have a day and night mobility advantage of about a factor of ten over armoured vehicles. A medium lift helicopter can carry twice the load and has a payload × speed product about ten times that of a five-ton truck. However they may remain weather-limited and demand a high level of maintenance and support.

Although tactical reconnaissance capacity will be improved and data handling technology will speed up systematic storage, retrieval and presentation of data, the problem of interpreting enemy intentions remains a task for the well-trained commander with the right intuition. Commanders lacking these qualities will, in spite of new technology, realize only too late what is about to happen. It remains to be seen whether improvements in surveillance will prove sufficient to allow full exploitation of increased tactical mobility.

Whether the inherent tactical mobility of future forces results in highly mobile warfare could, however, depend more upon the relative emphasis given to tactical mobility and fire-power in future force structures and in the forces on both sides in a given battle. Sufficient densities of new indirect-fire, anti-tank and air-defence weapons would cause loss rates in excess of the capacity to reinforce and replace front units, and thus hold-down of mobile operations. With sufficient priority on highly mobile weapons, personnel and supply carriers, and at the expense of fire-power, highly mobile operations would succeed.

Since new weapons technology so extensively hinges on reception of electromagnetic energy by target seekers, guidance receivers, surveillance equipment and radio receivers, injection by the enemy of false signals or noise may reduce the performance of new systems. The character of most of the systems is such that if deception or jamming succeeds, the effectiveness of the system is drastically reduced. Decoys, deceptive signals, passive measures (such as camouflage) or noise could cause normally highly accurate missiles to miss the target completely. Jamming could reduce the effective coverage of radars significantly. The balance between new systems, countermeasures and counter-countermeasures could be highly dynamic, reducing a highly effective system one day to mediocrity the next. The effect of being caught by surprise in this field could be equally consequential as being tactically surprised.

The capacity to inflict losses at high rates, to manoeuvre with high tactical mobility, to conduct combat with integrated arms teams day and night, to achieve surprise by exploiting the broader range of tactical and technical options is likely to make combat more intense. Human endurance will, however, limit the length of periods over which hard physical activity and, perhaps more important, ingenuity and initiative can be maintained. Unless front-line units worn down by intense combat can be replaced at sufficient rates, future wars may consist of relatively brief periods of highly intensive combat followed by periods with considerably lower intensity combat and rebuilding of strength in the combat zone. Adverse weather, e.g. snow, heavy rain, thaw, etc. will, however, impair the ability of men and several types of equipment to perform effectively and reduce combat intensity.

The Theatre

More than ever, the side best able to exploit theatre-level reserves and support will have a decisive advantage. The high loss rates and strains of future combat will require frequent replacement of front-line forces with reserves. The increased accuracy of weapon systems will reduce the tonnage of ammunition supplies to each weapon, but increased mobility will increase the strain on the fuel supply system.

The pressure of time on management and movement of reserves and support will increase the importance of early information about enemy movements and concentration of forces. Theatre-level surveillance will undoubtedly draw on national satellite surveillance. SIGINT and ELINT, possibly satellite-borne, would probably provide some information about where and when interesting activities take place. Weather satellites could be used to provide information about periods with acceptable cloud cover, which, because of the rather high look-angles of surveillance satellites, probably would occur more often than traditional cloud statistics would imply. Cloud-cover permitting, electro-optical sensors in satellites should, day and night, be able to detect and locate movement of large forces. But satellites would not be invulnerable to enemy action and interference, be it physical or electromagnetic.

In spite of the increased capacity of strategic and theatre surveillance systems to provide good and timely intelligence on enemy activities, and the capability of modern communications and data handling technology to speed up data processing and presentation, delays cannot be avoided. The ability of the commander and his staff to interpret the situation may, however, be the critical element in the timely initiation of reinforcement and support operations.

Reserves and support on the move represent a great number of individual targets. Even with precision-guided weapons, many weapons would have to penetrate air defences to achieve a significant damage level. The effectiveness of future air defence systems and the related cost of weapons and weapon platforms could well make this option less attractive than an attack on infrastructure supporting reinforcement and support operations.

The high and practically range-independent accuracy of precision-guided weapons and their capacity to hit selected critical parts of a complex target make them well suited for attacks against road and rail bridges, centres controlling rail and road traffic, air traffic and airfield control centres, computer-based military management systems, fuel storage facilities, the general electricity supply system, etc. The smaller number of such targets would make it possible for the attack to accept higher losses to achieve destruction. The effect would not be to stop reserves and support, but the resulting confusion and reorganization would take time and the rates of movement would be impaired.

In spite of steadily improving infrastructure and better surveillance capability, the effectiveness of precision-guided weapons against key infrastructure targets could well become the crucial factor in reinforcement and support operations.

The Strategic Level

None of the nations likely to become involved in a major East–West confrontation maintains sufficient combat-ready forces in the theatre to fight a war successfully. The Warsaw Pact may have enough forces in East Europe for an initial attack, but it appears unlikely that they would initiate a military contest in Central Europe without comprehensive and lengthy development of their war potential. On neither side will modern technology markedly reduce the length of the process of transition from peace to war posture. The risks of escalation to nuclear war could even entail more comprehensive preparations than before previous wars in this area.

The increased strategic surveillance capacity would enhance markedly the probability of detecting several of the measures which would have to precede major military initiatives. Activation of commands and the trimming of forces and testing of material being made combat-ready could hardly be accomplished without radiation of electromagnetic energy typical of the equipment involved and likely to be detected by ground or satellite-borne ELINT and SIGINT equipment. Electro-optical satellite surveillance would detect movement of large forces and possibly other activities. As time would be less critical at this level, cloud cover would be a lesser problem. Over-the-horizon radars and modern airborne surveillance radars would detect significant deviations from normal air activity, and ocean surveillance systems should at least be able to monitor some of the fleet deployments which probably would precede initiation of hostilities in Central Europe.

Although new technology applied to strategic surveillance will increase the capacity to monitor closer to real time most of the indicators critical to preparations for war, the major problem will be, as has been the case several times before in history, to interpret the various elements of warning correctly and initiate appropriate measures sufficiently early. The preparedness and mobility of the minds of those who have the heavy responsibility of making decisions of such gravity might again be more critical for the initiation of well-timed reactions than incomplete intelligence.

The Offence/Defence Balance

Focusing on Europe and new conventional weapons technology, the point of prime interest is the implication of this technology for NATO's capacity to maintain a credible conventional defence posture and the Warsaw Pact's capacity to attack with conventional weapons and reach its objectives quickly. In this paper the offence/ defence balance means the balance between these two capacities.

It has been a popular notion that precision-guided weapons will substantially favour NATO's ability to maintain a credible conventional defence against such attacks. Overly simplified, the argument has been that one precision-guided anti-tank weapon costing perhaps $7,000 (*TOW*) will be able with high probability to destroy a tank costing about $1m. The low cost of anti-tank weapons would allow NATO to establish a formidable defence by dispersed deployment of such weapons in great numbers.

However, future capacity to locate firing weapons quickly and to produce effective counterfire would stand a good chance of destroying the fire-control unit that fired the weapon. This costs $80,000. Furthermore, in attacks on a defence consisting of numbers of potentially highly effective anti-tank weapons, it is unlikely that the Warsaw Pact would not use strong area-weapon fire support to suppress anti-tank weapons similar to *TOW* which had no physical protection for weapon and crew. Protection could be provided by covered weapon positions or by mounting the weapon on an armoured vehicle. As the cost of an armoured vehicle with fire-control and precision-guided anti-tank weapons would be close to that of a tank, there would hardly be any cost difference between the anti-tank weapon and its prime target. Because of the number of positions required, protection by prepared covered positions would be time consuming and rather inflexible.

Although the cost figures differ, the need for physical protection of the new light and highly effective air defence systems will similarly raise the cost per unit fielded to a level no longer negligible in comparison with the cost of the airborne vehicles they are to fight. Furthermore, successful defence will require the defender to engage in covering operations and counter-attack which will require fire-power, mobility and protection at about the same level as that of the attacking forces, at corresponding cost. The number of precision-guided anti-tank and air defence weapons likely to be fielded might, therefore, well be several times less than the numbers suggested by mere consideration of net weapon cost. However, as the attacker would be more exposed, the defence would normally have the advantage of the first engagement with a highly effective weapon. On the other hand, new target acquisition equipment will probably contribute more towards quick and effective counterfire from the attacker than it will to the effectiveness of defensive weapons. Considering a single engagement in isolation, the net effect might well be in favour of defence. But a successful defence would normally involve counter-attacks, which would reverse the advantage. However, there can hardly be any doubt that loss rates in future engagements will be high.

Helicopters may offer a substantial increase in tactical mobility which could be as important to the offence/defence balance as precision-guided weapons. By overflying fixed defences, helicopters provide an opportunity for seizing objectives in depth. In the defence, it might be possible to speed the concentration of fire-power against a breakthrough or assist in counter-attacks. There will, however, be a cost penalty. An attack helicopter would probably cost two-to-three times as much as a tank; a medium lift helicopter one-to-five times.

The relative emphasis in future forces on tactical mobility versus density and effectiveness of fire-power could well be a crucial factor in the problem of whether new technology will favour offence or defence. If mobility were to dominate, battles could become highly dynamic and increase the probability that the attacker, having the initiative, would achieve an early success. If density and effectiveness of fire-power were to dominate over mobility, battles could become rather static and reduce the danger of quick Warsaw Pact attacks penetrating to great depth.

Surprise has, however, often been the deciding factor in battles. The range of new weapons, sensors and other types of material, together with the almost dramatic effects of successful electronic countermeasures, may provide the basis for a much broader spectrum of technical and tactical options for both offence and defence. The ability to exploit the options created by new technology may be at least as important as the technology itself.

As the Warsaw Pact would have the initiative in the opening phases of a war in Central Europe, its reserves and support could be brought forward even before the attack. The transportation infrastructure in Eastern Europe is somewhat less sophisticated than its Western counterpart and it might therefore survive an attack rather better. Important parts of Warsaw Pact forces are equipped to cross water without the use of bridging equipment. NATO movement of reserves and support would also be impaired by the confusion caused by destruction of critical nodes in, for instance, the electricity supply system in the densely populated and highly integrated societies of the West. The Warsaw Pact would also have the advantage of pre-planning its interdiction operations. Being the attacker, however, they would require considerably more forces and support brought forward. Nevertheless, in the early phases of a war, precision-guided weapons might favour the Warsaw Pact's capacity to slow down NATO reserves and support rather than *vice versa*.

In NATO the process of calling up reserves, readying material, making forces combat-ready, transportation to the theatre, etc., would of necessity take a relatively long time measured in the time scale of a highly intense and possibly mobile war. Important parts of the forces would even have to cross the Atlantic. Unless the process were initiated a long time before the attack, Warsaw Pact interdiction operations as discussed above could pose a serious threat to the successful completion of the process.

On the other hand, Warsaw Pact preparations for war would involve much the same processes and also take considerable time. The advances being made in systems for strategic surveillance will clearly favour NATO and tellingly increase its capacity for timely monitoring of indicators of Warsaw Pact preparations for attack. The intelligence picture would, however, not be complete, and uncertainties would exist. Only the tragedy of a war would prove whether NATO could exploit the advantage of much better intelligence and react in time. However, the knowledge in the Warsaw Pact of NATO's significantly increased strategic intelligence capacity would in itself probably be an important deterrent. So far, the assumption has been equal access for both sides to new weapons technology. If, however, one side had a definite lead in most of the sectors of conventional weapons technology, there can be hardly any doubt that the offence/defence balance would shift in favour of that side. If they so decide, the NATO nations have the scientific and technological traditions and the

industrial flexibility and capacity to gain a clear lead.

Can NATO Maintain an Advantage?

It has been argued, probably correctly, that level-headed adaptation of new technology weapons and equipment would give more defence per dollar. But it does not therefore follow that a future NATO defence taking advantage of new weapons technology will cost less than the present defence. If the Warsaw Pact were to continue strengthening and re-equipping their forces (and there is no sign to the contrary), NATO's problem would be to maintain a conventional offence/defence balance. In all probability this can be achieved at less cost with new weapons technology than without. But, disregarding inflation, it would cost more than today's defence.

Also disregarding inflation, the cost of material increases steadily as a consequence of more capability being built into weapons and equipment. A limited Norwegian analysis suggests that, for relatively simple equipment, there will be an average annual increase of about 2·5 per cent, disregarding inflation, in the cost of conventional material intended to perform the same functions. Over a generation (20 years) this means that costs will increase by a factor of 1·6. The corresponding figures for the technologically most advanced types of material, e.g. fighter aircraft, guided weapons, etc., appears to be about 5 per cent and a factor of 2·6. The analysis also shows that the average lifetime of material has been twenty-four years and that the average fraction of the defence budget used for acquisition of material has been about 25 per cent.

On the basis of these figures some rough estimates may be made of the necessary budget requirements to maintain the same volume of material under different assumptions about average lifetime and the cost increase of material due to more advanced technology. Assuming that, disregarding inflation, the annual operating cost of the defence budget remains constant, the defence budget would have to increase by 3 per cent annually to allow a reduction of average lifetime from twenty-four to eighteen years. Investments in material would have to increase from 25 to 27 per cent of the defence budget. This assumes an average annual increase of

2·5 per cent in material acquisition costs due to more advanced technology. If this annual cost increase were 4 per cent and the lifetime twenty years, the defence budget would have to increase by about 10 per cent annually, and the portion spent on new material would have to increase from 25 to about 32 per cent of the total budget. However, if twenty-four years average lifetime were acceptable, and the annual increase due to technology were 2·5 per cent, then 0·6 per cent increase in the defence budget would suffice.

In the past, the unavoidable consequence of new technology and increased turn-over of material has always been some increase in annual operating costs. The ever-increasing standard of living, reduction of working hours per week, etc., in the industrialized nations will also increase the costs of maintaining a given force posture, i.e. increase the annual operating costs. Even

disregarding inflation, the budget estimates above are, therefore, on the low side.

There is no basis for firm opinions about the future annual cost increase of material due to more advanced technology. If the average life-time should have to be reduced, or if the annual cost increase due to more advanced technology should be above 2·5 per cent, the necessary annual increase in defence budgets to maintain numerical strength could be beyond what some nations so far have been willing to accept.

There can be hardly any doubt that a level-headed lead in new conventional weapons technology would increase NATO's ability to maintain a credible conventional defence posture. As, however, geography remains the same, new weapons technology seems to impose on NATO another re-examination of the trade-offs between quality and quantity.

Air and Anti-Air Capabilities

DONALD A. HICKS

Introduction

For many years the West has witnessed the emergence of the Soviet/Warsaw Pact capability for breakthrough attack on the Central Front of NATO. Evidence that this overall capability is maturing is clear both in Soviet military exercises and in the recently accelerated development and deployment of Soviet and Warsaw Pact conventional forces.

The success of a Soviet breakthrough attack will depend upon the co-ordinated execution of a number of critical missions; successful defence against the attack will require timely NATO action to disrupt and prevent the accomplishment of these missions. Among other things NATO will need air and anti-air forces which have the capability to:

(a) engage and destroy raids of large numbers of enemy aircraft, flying at low altitudes, in all weather;

(b) suppress or otherwise negate heavy Warsaw Pact air defences; and

(c) locate, engage, and negate Soviet ground manoeuvre units (including tanks, field artillery, supply trucks, etc.) at night, in adverse weather conditions and in the presence of heavy defences.

This article will discuss applications of new technology which can support concepts of operation designed to achieve these capabilities.

At the outset it is important to keep in mind the obvious fact that the tactical air activities must be closely linked to the ground war. A major objective will be to improve the ground-war environment by achieving and maintaining at least local air superiority, by providing airborne reconnaissance and by providing close air support.

Defining the Task

Air operations supporting a Warsaw Pact breakthrough attack on the NATO Central Front demand highly co-ordinated, low-level penetration of a large number of aircraft in bad weather. These penetrating aircraft will be targeted against high-value NATO targets, including bases, supply concentrations and nuclear assets. On the ground the Warsaw Pact will deploy many concentrated manoeuvre units which will be heavily defended. The NATO challenge is to provide a large and significant increase in the capability to counter these raids, these manoeuvre units and these defences.

Warsaw Pact Frontal Aviation

During the last ten years there has been a substantial increase in both the number and capabilities of Warsaw Pact air forces. In the period from 1955 to 1970, first-generation Pact aircraft were retired at a rate which balanced the introduction of second-generation aircraft. This resulted in a numerically constant force structure. Since 1970, however, Warsaw Pact forces have been introducing third-generation Soviet aircraft at about four times the retirement rate of the previous generation of aircraft. This is resulting in a build-up from about 3,500 aircraft in 1970 to a force level which could exceed 6,000 by 1980. At the same time Soviet fighter and fighter-bomber aircraft have improved qualitatively. This qualitative improvement enables the expansion of the Warsaw Pact tactical air mission from one of air defence and close air support to one which also encompasses interdiction strikes deep into NATO territory. Thus the Warsaw Pact Frontal Aviation can now augment the Soviet bomber force in attacks on Western targets, especially in low-altitude escort and defence suppression roles. The new *Fitter* (Su-20) and *Fencer* (Su-19) aircraft could reach most of the NATO bases in Western Europe while flying at low altitude to improve their survivability. In later Soviet aircraft design the close, manoeuvring combat role has not been emphasized, but the aircraft have achieved performances in intercept and interdiction comparable to NATO aircraft. Overall, Warsaw Pact combat aircraft now in service demonstrate increased range and payload capability, together with increased thrust-to-weight ratio. For example, there have been substantial increases in the range of Soviet search and tracking radars and of their air-to-air missiles with radar or infra-red homing capabilities. In short, there has been a substantial increase in the threat to air bases and other high-value NATO targets. The greatly improved penetration and interdiction capability of the Warsaw Pact air forces is a major challenge that must be countered.

Pact Ground-force Capabilities
The Soviet Union must rapidly reinforce second-echelon forces to exploit breakthroughs achieved by first-echelon forces in their initial assaults. NATO tactical air units must be able to locate, engage and destroy (or disable) these Soviet ground units swiftly and completely enough to affect significantly the outcome of the ground battle. Attacks by NATO strike aircraft must be conducted at night, in bad weather, and in the presence of heavy defences.

Warsaw Pact Air Defences
Although the emphasis of Soviet tactical aircraft production has now shifted towards longer-range aircraft capable of extensive low-altitude operations, the Warsaw Pact force of short-range aircraft is expected to be maintained at current or higher levels. Pact countries maintain large inventories of short-range aircraft and air defence systems which they believe are sufficient to exact a prohibitive price from NATO attacks.

The Soviet ground-based air defence posture is particularly formidable when compared with that of NATO. Each Soviet division has about five times as many anti-aircraft guns and three to four times as many missiles as a NATO division. A typical deployment of surface-to-air missiles (SAM) in a Soviet army (three to four divisions) would be five batteries of SA-6, nine of SA-4, five of SA-8 and three of SA-2. In addition there are large numbers of SA-7 and of vehicle-mounted SA-9 launchers, and typically 80 batteries of anti-aircraft guns.

New Technologies
The defence problems faced by NATO must be overcome in an environment of essentially fixed defence budgets; solutions must therefore be low-cost, maximum use must be made of existing assets (aircraft, etc.) and investments in new technology must offer quantum improvements in capability for any given investment.[1]

Air Defence over NATO Territory
The threat to high-value NATO targets from large raids of Su-19 and Su-20 penetrating at low altitude under cloud cover must partly be countered by a numerically smaller force of NATO tactical aircraft. In order to engage and destroy many Pact aircraft, NATO tactical aircraft will require:

(a) *The ability to operate autonomously.* While an Airborne Warning and Control System (AWACS) or ground control can vector interceptors to the raid, it cannot be expected to control individual engagements during a dense raid.

(b) *An effective look-down capability (all weather and night).* NATO aircraft will engage the low-altitude penetrators from medium altitudes and must, therefore, have onboard radars capable of looking down through cloud cover and ground clutter.

(c) *Track-while-scan radar capability.* In the expected dense target environment, the aircraft radar and fire-control system must be capable of tracking one target while looking for others.

---

[1] Throughout this article reference will be made to new technology based upon Large Scale Integrated (LSI) micro-electronic components, micro-computer elements (micro-processor and memory), and advanced sensors. For a description of this technology see chapter by Charles Herzfeld below.

(d) *Small, lightweight, short- to medium-range air-to-air missiles with an active radar seeker*. A missile with a shoot-down capability must be carried on most of our NATO fighter aircraft. It must be affordable and compatible with small fighters. Each NATO aircraft must be equipped with many missiles which can be fired through cloud cover to home automatically on the target aircraft.

(e) *Onboard data processing and display system*. Extensive data can be available to the pilot, both from the onboard and external sources. We must provide sufficient data processing onboard the aircraft so that a single pilot can absorb required information while he is engaged in attacking enemy aircraft.

Autonomous Operation

Each defending NATO aircraft must be capable of destroying many enemy aircraft without external assistance. The Warsaw Pact will employ sophisticated electronic countermeasures (ECM), communication jamming and raid configuration control (spacing, timing, etc.), to enhance the survivability of their attacking aircraft. Existing Western technology, if exploited, can provide the NATO fighter pilot with an unprecedented amount of information and capability to support autonomous air-to-air engagement as well as to counter these defensive measures. The availability of large-scale integration (LSI) hardware permits onboard combination of extensive data bases, high-output sensors, complex data processing algorithms, and displays that are carefully engineered for quick recognition and comprehension by the pilot.

The impact of this new technology can best be described by examining a specific illustrative concept of operation during a Warsaw Pact attack. Many sources of information will continuously provide data which will signal an advent of an attack by enemy forces. For the purpose of this discussion the term 'combat operation centre' will be used to describe a node where data obtained in a given localized area of the front both by surveillance and from friendly sources is combined and processed in order to engage and disrupt these enemy forces.

Once a Warsaw Pact attack begins, information from many real-time sources will flow into the combat operations centre to be correlated and combined with the existing data base. In particular, radar systems will detect and then begin tracking the incoming Warsaw Pact air offensive.

NATO interceptors will be vectored towards the incoming Pact raid. At the same time, data from the combat operations centre can be communicated to a sophisticated onboard data processing system on each NATO aircraft. Prior to and during the actual engagement, these aircraft can also serve as an external input source to the combat operations centre. Tracking data from the onboard radar, parameter measurements from the ECM equipment, and formatted pilot assessments may be communicated to the centre from the aircraft. Control of each NATO aircraft will not be necessary. Further, subsequent defenders benefit from the most up-to-date and complete information on the Pact raid. Communication bandwidth requirements are minimized through the use of highly formatted digital data, communications preprocessors, and theatre-wide data format conventions (such as a common grid). Minimizing the bandwidth permits the employment of anti-jamming and data security techniques. It is feasible to put all this onboard the aircraft through the application of micro-electronics and micro-processors.

The onboard data processing system also handles the missile fire-control function, provides displays to aid the pilot in deciding how to engage the raid and which aircraft to attack, and afterwards, how to re-engage in the most effective manner. These features result in freeing the pilot from many of the tasks which currently fully occupy him, while significantly increasing his performance and eliminating his dependence upon one-on-one external intercept control.

More Effective Air-to-Air Missiles

The technology is at hand to build small, low-cost, all weather, air-to-air missiles at a size and cost which will permit their deployment on most (if not all) NATO aircraft. Each NATO fighter will be able to carry eight to ten missiles capable of shooting down enemy aircraft in bad weather, with little or no post-launch assistance from the fighter pilot. Micro-processors and large-capability digital memory onboard the missile will enable the use of a more capable radar seeker, a low-cost, strap-down inertial guidance system, and sophisticated tracking logic. Within a small, inexpensive package we can achieve the ability to fire down into clouds and ground clutter with increased accuracy and with greater autonomy from the launching aircraft.

The concept of operation described above, coupled with the new technology systems, can serve to improve significantly the ability of NATO fighters to defend against raids of low-flying Pact aircraft. Each NATO fighter will have an increased potential for quickly engaging and shooting down enemy aircraft as well as an improved chance to re-engage the raid. More enemy aircraft will be killed by each defender before the attacking aircraft reach their objective. The ability to fire missiles and promptly disengage will further improve fighter survivability, contributing to an increased exchange ratio.

NATO Ground-Based Air Defences
Because there are insufficient numbers of them, ground-based air defences deployed in NATO cannot be expected at the moment to contribute significantly to the interception of concentrated air attacks against NATO air bases and other high-value resources. *Nike-Hercules* at fixed sites are highly vulnerable to initial strikes specifically intended to reduce NATO air-defence capability. *Hawk* is somewhat more mobile but can be located by electronic and photographic reconnaissance. Both systems are vulnerable to anti-radiation missile attack and vulnerable to saturation under attack by multiple fighter bombers. The fundamental design approach, based upon target-dedicated radar illuminators, severely restricts rate of fire available either for self-defence or for interception of the primary attacking force. While the Soviet SAM have similar vulnerability their overwhelming number limit their susceptibility to saturation.

Introduction of *Patriot* and new short-range air defences such as *Roland*, which are more capable than their Soviet counterparts, will improve the situation considerably. Yet the increased rate of fire and high effectiveness of *Patriot* result from high-power sophisticated radars which can be fielded only in limited numbers. As a consequence, many of these radars will undoubtedly become prime initial targets along with *Nike-Hercules*. A further problem is that *Patriot*, *Hawk*, and *Nike-Hercules* were conceived when Warsaw Pact

aircraft were not capable of deep low-altitude penetrations. Irregular terrain, particularly in Southern Germany will restrict the interception range actually achievable in these nominally long-range air defence systems. Increased deployment of short-range air defence would overcome this problem, but the numbers necessary to equip the field armies, protect each high-value NATO asset and deploy along possible, or at least probable penetration routes are likely to be prohibitively expensive.

In this context, fighter aircraft provide an attractive solution to the problem. They can be vectored by AWACS and ground control to the actual penetration routes, thus avoiding the otherwise prohibitive cost of prepositioning defences at all possible locations. Equipped with modern look-down radars and air-to-air missiles, fighter aircraft are not defeated by terrain masking.

One final comment should be made concerning ground-based defences. As a consequence of the Warsaw Pact capability to concentrate large numbers of aircraft for low-altitude penetrations to key NATO resources located in rear positions – even in the United Kingdom – a ground-based air defence system is now needed which is intended specifically for point defence. This system must have unrestricted rate of fire. Each of its weapons must have an unprecedentedly high kill effectiveness since any single surviving aircraft or missile target could do considerable damage. The new generation of short-range systems based on command-to-line-of-sight are limited in rate of fire, though much improved compared to earlier systems, and they are liable to have their effectiveness impaired by evasive target manoeuvring. However, as with air-to-air missiles, the technologies of active radar seekers and microprocessors promise new air defence missiles capable of autonomous operation following launch, high accuracy independent of target manoeuvre, and improved survivability through remote location of fire-control elements, whether conventional or multistatic radars.

NATO Air Attack on Concentrated Pact Manoeuvre Units
Warsaw Pact ground manoeuvre units must be deployed for the breakthrough attack, and they

will present concentrated targets to NATO offensive air forces. Tactical air will play an important role in negating these targets. Locating Pact manoeuvre units at night and in bad weather will be a difficult task. Attacking aircraft will have to penetrate heavy area and point defences, and the Soviet Union will use ECM to disrupt NATO operations. Finally, all targets will not be of equal value to the enemy's offensive and it will be difficult to make informed selections as to which targets are to be attacked.

The NATO air offensive on Pact ground manoeuvre units is conceptually similar to the air defence task described earlier. A surveillance system must acquire, locate and to some extent classify and evaluate clusters of targets. Strike aircraft must be directed towards these clusters. These aircraft must be capable of autonomous (or almost autonomous) operations, since continuous external control is not feasible. Each must be able to accomplish its mission despite heavy defences, and each must be equipped with weapons which take advantage of the dense target environment to provide the potential for many target kills per sortie.

As in the air-to-air mission above, a rather specific concept of operation will be described to illustrate the potential application of new technology. The concept begins with the combat operations centre. This centre correlates all source data on which to base the assignment of a surveillance aircraft to a general area. This aircraft may operate outside the range of enemy ground-based air defences. Onboard a multi-mode, Synthetic Aperture Radar (SAR) provides target acquisition, location, and assessment.

Processing SAR data is one of the most demanding sensor data-processing tasks. Literally billions of bits of data must be processed before it is possible to extract any useful information. In the past instantaneous 'real time' processing of SAR data onboard an aeroplane was totally unfeasible. As a result vast amounts of data had to be communicated from the aircraft to a ground processing facility using extremely vulnerable wide-band communication links. Even with a ground-based processing centre, it was generally not feasible to process SAR data in real time. Significant delays in providing useful information resulted. With new micro-electronics technology for extensive data processing, onboard memory, and radar preprocessors, real time SAR sur-

veillance is now feasible. The same data processing technology permits the employment of sophisticated moving target indication, change detection and pattern recognition algorithms to acquire, select and describe the manoeuvre-unit target complexes. Target co-ordinates and other target data are communicated to the combat operations centre and to NATO offensive tactical air units. Each NATO attack aircraft is assigned a target – the centroid of a grouping of individual manoeuvre elements – and the data relating to this target is stored onboard. To minimize the communications and the data-processing burden, target co-ordinates are computed in a common grid system to an accuracy of less than one hundred metres.

The attack aircraft must now navigate accurately to the point where it will deliver its ordnance: in this case wide-area munitions. Accurate navigation is achieved by using a number of redundant systems such as ground-based calibration beacons, Global Positioning Satellite System (GPS) or Joint Tactical Information Distribution System (JTIDS) together with an onboard inertial system. The onboard data processing system allows the combination of navigation inputs and the update of the inertial system. Through the use of more sophisticated processing algorithms it is possible to rely on less expensive and less mechanically complex strap-down inertial systems. The onboard processor also computes the precise velocity vector and time for weapon release.

The wide-area munition is a canister filled with submunitions that are deployed in a pattern. The pilot in the delivery aircraft is not required to acquire a special target, and once launched the wide-area munition deployment canister is independent of the delivering aircraft. One form of a wide-area munition would deploy submunitions which have individual terminal guidance, so that each can search and home on an individual target within the dense target cluster. The localization of the centroid of the target elements and the navigation of the attacking aircraft must be accomplished with an accuracy compatible with the area of influence of the submunition. The feasibility of a low-cost submunition with sufficient capability to sense, acquire and home on a target stems from advances in LSI electro-optical sensor arrays as well as low-cost micro-processors.

In situations where the target complex is moving, co-ordinate updates from the surveillance platform may be required. Use of a common grid system and a formatted digital communication link to the attacking aircraft (as in the air-to-air case described earlier) minimizes the amount of actual data which must be transmitted. This permits employment of anti-jamming techniques. Much of this 'data compression' is feasible as a result of the onboard micro-processor.

Penetrating Soviet Defences

The Warsaw Pact will have an imposing array of defences that will exact a crippling toll from NATO aircraft unless countered. One obvious approach is to use stand-off weapons, so as to remain outside the range of SA-6 and even SA-4. The development of an inexpensive, stand-off, wide-area munition with sufficient accuracy, range and payload represents a formidable technical challenge. While such low-cost, stand-off weapons will be feasible, approaches which permit the strike aircraft itself to penetrate to the munition release point with reasonable attrition must also be pursued.

One way to reduce attrition is to use attack profiles that reduce the exposure time of the delivery aircraft and tend to saturate the enemy defences, and the combat operations centre described earlier will help in this. Individual aircraft exposure time can be reduced greatly by concentrating large-scale attacks in a particular area and in a particular time slot to saturate the defences, and by then releasing launch-and-leave area type munitions. The possibility of using a few aircraft on 'search and destroy' missions seems out of the question; again, the advances in an information/common grid system (such as those inherent in JTIDS), coupled with advanced area type munitions, will underwrite this concept.

Offensive jamming will help delay the point in time when the defences start reacting to NATO attacks and will decrease the interval available for the defences to acquire, track and attack one of the NATO fighters. Onboard ECM packages (containing sensors capable of detecting radar over a broad frequency band and the necessary data processing) can be geared to jam specific radars automatically. Miniaturized electronic packages also make possible small, low-cost

expendable drones that can simulate the radar return of attacking aircraft and can also act as distributed jammers. These drones also act as decoys to thin out the enemy attack against NATO aircraft, and by jamming they confuse enemy defences.

We must also work hard on a concept in which any enemy radar that emits for more than a few seconds can be attacked quickly and effectively. This presents a great technical challenge in information processing; a particular radar must be singled out from a large number of radars for accurate attack, quickly and without ambiguity. Measuring the difference in time of arrival at three different inter-related platforms is one approach, but the acquisition of the basic data in the presence of possible Soviet jamming and the processing of this data so that real radars are not missed and false targets are not attacked remain a technical challenge.

Attack of enemy radars can also be accomplished by a small remotely piloted vehicle. This is a very low-cost vehicle which carries a combat-proven radar seeker and a small warhead optimized for attack of mobile ground radars. It is used to harass enemy radars by loitering in the combat area and attacking selected radars. It can be constructed of moulded plastic for large-volume production and is powered by an inexpensive gasoline engine. Development of such a weapon system may evolve as a joint programme between the United States and West Germany.

Summing Up

Most of the systems discussed are feasible as the result of recent advances in micro-electronics and micro-computer technology, as well as advances in radar and electro-optical sensor subsystems. In many cases the performance, reliability and cost of these advanced technology systems have been demonstrated. Some are already under development; others exist as devices and components, requiring integration at some later date into a workable system. Still others are conceptual only and may prove not to be cost-effective or practical.

Throughout the discussion examples of concepts of operation have been described along with the systems which support these concepts. This underlines a most important point: technology alone cannot be used to 'paper over' a lack of an operational concept. Capabilities must derive from a thorough examination of operational objectives from the top down– threat environment, concept of operation, and the resulting systems and associated technologies which enable these concepts. It is, of course, an interactive process but one often by-passed in favour of working on new technology for its own sake, without a central, integrated purpose.

The concepts of operation described in this article are reasonable, but certainly not unique. Other concepts of operations would lead to a need for different technical systems. It seems certain, however, that opportunities for application of new and emerging Western technology, such as described, will enable NATO forces to increase their qualitative advantages over Warsaw Pact forces.

Command, Control and Communications

C. M. HERZFELD

Comminications, Command and Control (C^3) are the sinews and nerves of military power. They are poorly understood, rarely appreciated, often blamed for military failures. But great military leaders pay meticulous attention to them, use their own C^3 assets carefully and fully exploit their enemies' weaknesses in this area.

Let me give a few examples of the importance of C^3. It is likely that one of the problems the British Navy had in the Battle of Jutland was a failure of C^3/I (that is C^3 plus Intelligence, especially of the operational, tactical kind). There was inadequate surveillance, inadequate use of the available surveillance data, inadequate communication to the Commander, inadequate instruction to and control of the forces from the Commander. Another, more recent example of the importance of C^3 comes from the Battle of the Atlantic in World War II. The German C^3 of the submarine force was vulnerable to exploitation: the traffic was read by the Allies, and the locations of emitters determined. To take a much older example: the Charge of the Light Brigade was in a real sense a C^3 failure.

C^3 is a sensitive area, in matters of policy issues and of security and secrecy. We are therefore fortunate to have a number of very useful references available to the public; this summary depends on them heavily. Rear Admiral Sir Arthur Hezlett's excellent book *The Electron and Sea Power* (London: Peter Davies, 1975) describes very well, in practical terms, the uses of C^3, with special emphasis on naval matters, though the broad principles apply to other aspects of warfare. The Annual Report of the US Defence Department for FY 1978 by Secretary Donald Rumsfeld described US policies and programmes well and the Report by the C^3 Panel of the US House Armed Services Committee of 18 February 1977 discusses a number of current problems and issues. (Naturally the discussion given of C^3 in this summary conveys only my own views, not those of the US Government, nor those of my employer.)

This summary concentrates on issues and problems involving higher military and civilian echelons of command. C^3 is required, in one form or another, in all levels of conflict, from a low-level crisis to all-out nuclear war. It is probably not useful to make a sharp distinction between non-nuclear war and nuclear war. To be sure, at the nuclear end of the spectrum the consultation and release procedures have special demands on the C^3 system, but these are really more differences of degree than of kind. C^3 systems should survive into and through nuclear war. At the other, 'non-nuclear', end of the spectrum the C^3 systems must always be ready for a transition to nuclear war. There are some discernible differences, but this article does not explore these in detail.

Definitions of Command and Control, and Communications

A useful, though not unique, way to proceed is to start with some official definitions. These are taken from Publication 1 of the US Department of Defense (authorized by the Joint Chiefs of Staff):

Command and Control:
The exercise of authority and direction by a properly designated commander over assigned forces in the accomplishment of his mission.

Command and control functions are performed through an arrangement of personnel, equipment, communications, facilities and procedures which are employed by a commander in planning, directing, co-ordinating and controlling forces and operations in the accomplishment of his mission.

Note especially the concepts of arrangement, procedures, planning, directing, co-ordinating, controlling. These are essentially software matters that do not depend exclusively or even primarily on hardware.

Communications:
A method or means of conveying information of any kind from one person or place to another, except by direct unassisted conversation or correspondence through non-military postal agencies.

In recent years the concept C^3/I has developed in the US. This operational type of intelligence is crucial for the full exploitation of modern weapons technology. Unfortunately target acquisition, identification and designation have actually fallen behind weapons technology, so that the full capabilities of, for example, precision-guided munitions and cruise missiles are difficult to use at the moment. Again, some of the new technologies discussed below will make major improvements possible.

C^3 connects the decision-makers with their information sources as well as with the forces that execute the orders and fight. In turn, results and assessments are fed back. These functions are largely hidden and unappreciated. Everyone knows that men, tanks, guns, ships and aeroplanes matter. These are counted, their numbers debated, their cost analysed. But none of them can be effective without C^3.

NATO C^3 Problems and Issues
Current NATO C^3 capabilities are severely limited because of a number of historical factors, such as the highly 'national' structures of the C^3 elements, much outmoded equipment and lack of appreciation of the crucial significance of C^3 for combat effectiveness. There are also serious shortcomings in target acquisition and in battle management. Many of the existing C^3 systems are not interoperable, which makes proper co-ordination of different national forces, as well as of land, air and naval arms, extremely difficult.

NATO communications systems involved exhibit the classical weaknesses of such systems – too many can be spoofed (by introduction of false messages); too many are vulnerable to electronic jamming, too many are vulnerable to exploitation (reading of text or locating of emitters) and too many are vulnerable to physical destruction. The command and control systems suffer from inadequate, inflexible procedures, and tend to fail 'hard' rather than 'soft', that is gradually. These systems also need more testing for readiness.

These problems cannot be solved in a definitive way, but an evolutionary long-range process can be started which would gradually improve NATO's C^3. This process can be helped greatly by some new technologies which are becoming available. However, it must be appreciated that C^3 is not a luxury – something that can be cut with impunity or sensibly 'traded' for combat equipment. It is essential for true military effectiveness.

C^3 is not cheap and it is at present highly manpower-intensive and very expensive to maintain. New technology well certainly reduce the manpower requirements for C^3 and, for a given cost, will be easier to maintain and to operate. But the C^3 abilities that are really needed will cost a good deal. Hence the balance of expenses for combat forces versus C^3 must be re-examined.

New Technologies that Matter
Two kinds of technologies matter for C^3. One kind has to do with the forces and their armaments. Faster aircraft need better C^3, more mobile forces need mobile C^3, cruise missiles will be able to make use of better C^3, and so on. New weapons technologies will allow forces to be dramatically more effective – but only if supported with better C^3. New technologies also make it easier to *build* and *use* C^3 systems, and it is the C^3 related technologies that have probably made the most dramatic advances in the last twenty years.

Of all the key technologies for C^3, microelectronics is without question the most important, and it will continue to develop rapidly. Next are probably communications satellites, while software technologies (such as netting of computers, netting of tactical units and techniques of programming called Higher Order

41

Languages and Structured Programming) will also be important. In the long run the use of Fibre Optics technology will become extremely significant. Each of these technologies will be described briefly.

The speed of development of micro-electronics has been startling. (For the history and prospects of micro-electronics see *Science*, Vol. 195, 18 March 1977.) In the 1950s the transistor became available, eventually replacing the vacuum tube. In the early 1960s integrated circuits consisting of some ten transistors became available. The late 1960s saw the arrival of what is now called medium-scale integration (MSI) with several hundred transistors on one chip of substrate, and now large-scale integration (LSI) is here, with about a thousand transistors on a 'chip' $\frac{1}{2}$ cm $\times \frac{1}{2}$ cm. And more is to come; very large-scale integration (VLSI) will have ten thousand transistors or more on a small chip, and the end is not in sight. At the same time the speed of these devices is increasing and power consumption going down. As a consequence, a computer of the power of the first electronic computer (the 1948 *ENIAC*, which was built entirely with vacuum tubes and filled several large rooms) can now be built – using a micro-processor – small enough so that it fits into a coat pocket. New high-capacity LSI memories will also be crucially important. The commercial uses of small, powerful, high-speed electronics for computers, watches, instrumentation and communication management is spreading rapidly and is just beginning to be introduced into military applications. It will have a most significant impact on military hardware: it will make them smaller, more reliable, and cheaper for *equivalent* capabilities.

Communications satellites are making rapid progress also. From a few telephone-channel-equivalents in the early 1960s, the technology will reach ten thousand telephone-channel-equivalents in the near future, and here too the end is not in sight. Increased capacity is important for C^3 applications partly because more information – such as pictures – can be communicated, partly because some of the capacity can be traded for robustness against jamming, so that a smaller volume of data can be sent through a jamming environment. This means that relatively robust, world-wide or theatre-wide communications systems can be achieved. A vulnerable segment of satellite communications is the ground segment – the ground stations and the communications links from the ground stations to the users. These can be hardened to some degree, and the whole system can be made more robust by proliferation of ground stations and ground communications links. Satellites are also vulnerable: they should be made more robust and increased in number.

Another important type of satellite system is the Global Positioning System (GPS) now under development in the United States. It will almost instantaneously provide users with highly accurate, three dimensional position information.

Netting of computers has been achieved. This allows pieces of large tasks to be distributed among many computers. More will be possible in the future. Netting of tactical electronic units is being developed in the United States in a series of systems called the Joint Tactical Information Distribution System (JTIDS). When fully developed this system will enable many mobile users to communicate with each other, determine their positions, exchange data, etc., all automatically and quite securely. Furthermore, this system will enable private and shared communications nets to operate together. This may enable several groups of users to have simultaneously available some 'allied' nets, while each group of users could also have its 'national' net.

Finally, the technology of Fibre Optics is maturing very fast. It is now possible to send light signals through thin glass or quartz fibres over long distances, and use these signals to communicate. It is also possible to make these fibres into small but strong cables. Therefore it is becoming feasible to send signals on land, under water and within structures such as ships and aircraft, using fibre optic technology. The advantages of doing so are considerable savings in weight, volume and – eventually – cost, as well as greatly reduced electro-magnetic interference, both accidental and intentional. This technology will soon become generally available.

All these advances together will make vastly greater performance available to new system designers and builders.

The most difficult tasks in modern electronics involve the programming of the electronics. Programmes must be written for tens or hundreds of thousands of instructions, differing greatly among each other, to be performed by equipments at a rate of millions of operations per second. This is a monumental task and it is becoming increasingly more complex and expensive. New approaches to programming involving Higher Order Languages make it possible to write consistent packages of instructions for ordered, structured sub-tasks. When fully implemented, these techniques will bring under control the large complex software problems of current systems, and also should lead to better understanding of the architectures of C^3 systems.

Approaches to Solving the C^3 Problem

The 'C^3 Problem' of NATO must be solved. A genuine solution will require significantly more technical collaboration and integration than has been achieved so far. In addition relatively more resources must be allocated to the C^3 sector of defence than has been traditionally the case. These are not primarily technical problems and so will not be elaborated here.

The chief weaknesses of the NATO C^3 system are that it is largely soft, and has a few key nodes which are easily destroyed; it does not have a reasonable degree of interoperability among different country or service components; it is not adequately secure against exploitation; and it tends to be rigid rather than adaptable to changing circumstances, in terms of capabilities, procedures and doctrines.

This is not the place to describe in detail an ideal future C^3 system for NATO except to point out that an evolutionary approach is needed. However, the new technologies outlined earlier should enable the Alliance to make significant moves in the right direction.

In the near future it should become possible to make the several satellite communications systems which are used by the Alliance and its members interoperable, and achieving this should be given urgent attention. Once this has become a reality, a proliferation of ground stations at many command posts, going down to corps, or perhaps even division level, would make the whole C^3 system very much more robust than it is now, both against physical destruction and jamming. A very serious effort should be mounted to make communications less easy to jam and exploit, micro-electronics being a key to a reasonably cost-effective solution.

C^3 will have to integrate all Command and Control assets as well as surveillance assets, targeting information and battle management. The technology of netting many 'subscribers' (users of a network) in a flexible way (allowing the establishment of specialized 'sub-nets' with different functions) is approaching reality. JTIDS, in one or several of its versions, will do an enormously improved job netting surveillance (such as AWACS) with command posts, with aircraft or land units, SAM, and in the future even with individual high precision weapons, such as remotely piloted vehicles (RPV) and cruise missiles.

The volume of communications that can be sent securely should be increased by factors of ten or more. A clear view of what is really needed is more important than technology. The technology is here (or will be available soon) to do whatever has to be done, but the doctrines need to be improved in a consistent and compatible manner.

Satellites are believed vulnerable, and so they are. However, ground stations are much more vulnerable, so they must be protected, increased in number and made mobile. In addition, however, some high-altitude aircraft serving as communication relays should be made available, to serve as back-up to satellites should these fail. (These aircraft relays might be RPV, avoiding the human limitations of time-on-station.)

Conclusion

In summary, the technology is here or under vigorous development to enable the Alliance in a number of years to achieve a C^3 system that could do the following:

— Have a hundred or more command headquarters at various echelons that are all linked to each other, their respective homelands and to the units they control. Many (most of these) should be mobile.

— The communications should use satellites, aircraft relays, point-to-point micro-wave and land lines (both dedicated and commercial).

— The communications could be secure against exploitation and robust to jamming.

— The C^3 system could integrate surveillance systems and command systems, down to individual high precision weapons.

ADE[

The following is a selection of those availabl[
£1.00 ($2.50) per copy, post free by surface [

No. 99. NUCLEAR WEAPONS AND CHINESE [
No. 100. INSURGENCY AND COUNTER-INSURG[
   by Anthony R. Wilkinson. Autumn 1973.
No. 101. SOVIET RISK-TAKING AND CRISIS B[
No. 102. FORCE IN MODERN SOCIETIES: ITS P[
   Annual Conference. Winter 1973.
No. 103. FORCE IN MODERN SOCIETIES: THE [
   Conference. Winter 1973.
No. 104. INDONESIA'S FUTURE AND SOUTH-E[
No. 105. NEW APPROACHES TO ARMS REDUC[
No. 106. NUCLEAR FORCES FOR MEDIUM POW[
   Geoffrey Kemp. Autumn 1974.
No. 107. NUCLEAR FORCES FOR MEDIUM POW[
   by Geoffrey Kemp. Autumn 1974.
No. 108. THE ALLIANCE AND EUROPE: PART[
   CHOICES by Roger Facer. Winter 1974/75.
No. 109. THE ALLIANCE AND EUROPE: PART[
   Winter 1974/75.
No. 110. AMERICAN FOREIGN POLICY IN THE [
No. 111. THE ARAB–ISRAEL WAR, OCTOBER [
   A. H. Farrar-Hockley. Winter 1974/75.
No. 112. DEFENCE BUDGETING: THE BRITISH[
No. 113. PROSPECTS FOR NUCLEAR PROLIFER[
No. 114. THE MIDDLE EAST AND THE INTERN[
   from the IISS Sixteenth Annual Conferen[
No. 115. THE MIDDLE EAST AND THE INTERN[
   Papers from the IISS Sixteenth Annual C[
No. 116. STRATEGIC DETERRENCE RECONSIDE[
No. 117. OIL AND INFLUENCE: THE OIL WEA[
No. 118. PRECISION-GUIDED WEAPONS by Jar[
No. 119. MILITARY POWER AND POLITICAL I[
   Vincent. Autumn 1975.
No. 120. THE ALLIANCE AND EUROPE: PART[
   Nerlich. Winter 1975/76.
No. 121. LIMITED NUCLEAR OPTIONS: DETER[
   Davis. Winter 1975/76.
No. 122. POWER AT SEA: PART I: THE NEW [
   ference. Spring 1976.
No. 123. POWER AT SEA: PART II: SUPER-PO[
   Conference. Spring 1976.
No. 124. POWER AT SEA: PART III: COMPE[
   Spring 1976.
No. 125. INDIA'S SECURITY IN THE 1980s by [
No. 126. NEW WEAPONS TECHNOLOGIES: DEF[
No. 127. DEFENDING THE CENTRAL FRONT: T[
No. 128. THE ARAB–ISRAEL DISPUTE: GREAT P[
No. 129. THE ALLIANCE AND EUROPE: PART VI: THE EUROPEAN PROGRAMME GROUP by D. C. R. Heyhoe.
   Winter 1976/77.
No. 130. NUCLEAR POWER AND WEAPONS PROLIFERATION by Ted Greenwood, George W. Rathjens and Jack
   Ruina. Winter 1976/77.
No. 131. THE SOVIET UNION AND THE PLO by Galia Golan. Winter 1976.
No. 132. AMERICAN SECURITY POLICY IN ASIA by Leslie H. Brown. Spring 1977
No. 133. THE DIFFUSION OF POWER: PART I: PROLIFERATION OF FORCE. Papers from the IISS Eighteenth
   Annual Conference. Spring 1977.
No. 134. THE DIFFUSION OF POWER: PART II: CONFLICT AND ITS CONTROL. Papers from the IISS Eighteenth
   Annual Conference. Spring 1977.
No. 135. BALKAN SECURITY by F. Stephen Larrabee. Spring 1977.
No. 136. OIL AND SECURITY: PROBLEMS AND PROSPECTS OF IMPORTING COUNTRIES by Edward N. Krapels
   Summer 1977.
No. 137. LATIN AMERICA IN WORLD POLITICS: THE NEXT DECADE by Gregory F. Treverton. Summer 1977.
No. 138. THE ROLE OF ARMS CONTROL IN THE MIDDLE EAST by Yair Evron. Autumn 1977.
No. 139. SEA POWER AND WESTERN SECURITY: THE NEXT DECADE by Worth H. Bagley. Winter 1977.
No. 140. THE FUTURE OF THE LAND-BASED FORCES by Colin Gray. Winter 1977.
No. 141. THE FUTURE OF ARMS CONTROL: PART I: BEYOND SALT II. Edited by Christopher Bertram.
   Spring 1978.
No. 142. THE SECURITY OF SOUTH-EAST ASIA by Bruce Grant. Spring 1978.
No. 143. A SEA OF TROUBLES? SOURCES OF DISPUTE IN THE NEW OCEAN REGIME by Barry Buzan. Spring 1978.

Discount rates are available for bulk orders of 11 or more Adelphi Papers of the same title.